TAKE CHARGE!
A guide to
FEELING GOOD

by
W. W. Johnston, Ed. D.

ACORN ENDEAVORS
PO Box 3336
Gresham, Oregon 97030

Second Printing - 1987

Cover created and owned by Sue Jansen

Library of Congress Catalog Card Number: 86-72631
ISBN 0-9619220-0-1 (wire binding)
ISBN 0-9619220-1-X (perfect binding)

Published by Acorn Endeavors, P.O. Box 3336
Gresham, Oregon 97030

TABLE OF CONTENTS

FOREWORD
by Jim Kern

Since 1972 Dr. W. W. Johnston, Wally, has walked with me as my teacher, as my counselor, as my colleague, and as my friend. I have grown immeasurably, changed consistently, and developed a more positive and accepting lifestyle through the influence of this man. Wally now offers this straight-forward synthesis of his life experiences to assist readers in finding healthy and positive strategies for more joyous living. I am sure that Wally would not want any of us to accept his word as our solution, but would prefer that we walk with him as he shares intriguing insights, personal experiences, exciting "Aha's," and lessons from those who have touched his life.

To know Wally is to love and respect him. In this concise and powerful book, Wally reveals himself to be well qualified to walk with us as we grow, to be a keen observer of life, and to be forever young. As our guide through these pages, Wally demonstrates his continuing growth, along with a desire to risk, to explore, and to question. He brings to us an exciting unity of concepts. We hear many hints behind these words that he will rejoice with us in our own growth and will share our joy as our own "clickers" are engaged.

Rarely in our lifetimes do any of us have a chance to present a friend and his ideas. I am proud and happy to introduce to you my friend, Wally Johnston. I am equally pleased to recommend this book as a pathway to your personal fulfillment and joy. I invite you now to enjoy your life's journey with this unique teacher, counselor and friend.

Jim Kern

My Plan For This Book

This is not a scholarly treatise on psychology or psychotherapy. This is a description of my personal and clinical experiences, my ideas, biases, learnings and convictions at this moment. I reserve the right to change my mind. I'm taking a look at my life. I've given myself permission to say what I please in any way that I please. I'm willing to share it with you. If you find it useful I'll get a 10% "commission" on your good feeling.

When the printer asked me how long I had been working on the book, I answered instantly, "all my life." But I've only been writing a few weeks. I'll be telling you something about me, some stories, opinions, essays, philosophy of life, quick fixes and affirmations.

In the introduction I will tell you about myself, my background and my experiences. Section I consists of stories about life and therapy and people who, by taking charge of their minds, were able to change the quality of their lives by changing their feelings.

Section II deals with the generally accepted falsehood which makes managing our feelings such a challenging task.

Section III on essays includes the opinions, biases and convictions which I now hold on subjects such as life, feelings and relationships.

Section IV is about a philosophy for life, those beliefs and assumptions on which we consciously or unconsciously base our decisions. I have traced some of my beliefs through the years, and offered a collection of quotations and sayings.

Section V includes quickie fixes and suggestions for smoothing out some of the minor snags in life.

Section VI on affirmations lists positive thoughts and visualizations for daily use in your project of taking charge and promoting your own good feelings.

Nothing about human life is more precious than that we can define our own purpose and shape our own destiny.

Norman Cousins in HUMAN OPTIONS

Introduction

TAKE CHARGE! My hope for you is that you will take charge of your life, your thinking and your feelings. There is just too much psychological pain in the world. Most of it is self-inflicted.

Psychological pain is an inside job. If you hurt, you have a problem. The answer will be related to your thinking and believing. By sharing my thinking I hope to stimulate **your** thinking so you can find an inside answer to your inside problem.

I really don't want to be your guru. I think that would be an insult to your own inner wisdom and uniqueness. I could be your teacher, or coach, but I'd rather be a consultant for you as you develop your self-management skills. It is proper for you to consider the counsel of the consultant, but the **final decision** rests with management. And when you "take charge" of your life, **you** are the manager and you are free to accept or reject my counsel. It's your life. The consequences are inevitably yours, and so the choice, appropriately, is yours.

I plan to share freely what I have learned in my varied experiences. I'm retired now and the nest is empty for the first time since October 1, 1945. I have the time to look back and synthesize (for myself) what I have learned. Maybe it will help you. I'll be pleased if you find my sharing useful.

My experience includes six years in private practice as a Licensed Consulting Psychologist in Minnesota, eleven years as a university professor and counselor at Winona State University in Minnesota, one year as a management psychologist in St. Louis, three years as a high school teacher/principal in Nebraska, two years as a superintendent of schools in Oregon, and 25 years military association, half of which was active duty in the Navy, Army Air Corps and the US Air Force.

In my most recent experience, as a psychologist, and earlier as a university counselor, I developed into a short-term therapist using a wide variety of techniques while emphasizing the effects of thoughts, beliefs, expectations and interpretations in the creation of one's own feelings.

At Winona State University I had an ideal opportunity. I taught theory half time and practiced what I "preached" the other half. I also had the freedom to continue my own education and develop courses which were relevant to life and living. Self Concept, Living with Dying, Stress & Biofeedback, and Human Relations were my favorites. I preferred the elective courses; it does something to the instructor and the students when a course is "required"–it has to be completed, but it doesn't have to be either interesting or relevant.

I like choices. That's why I chose Norman Cousins' quote on defining our own purpose and destiny. We can just let life happen and then react to it, or we can **take charge** and "go for it."

One caution is in order. If you are in an abusive, sick or toxic situation, take a look at that situation carefully before applying these techniques. Rather than blindly adjusting to a bad situation, you may want to be assertive or confrontational in order to try and change it. You may decide that the situation is beyond repair, or detrimental to your physical or emotional health. Then choosing to escape may be the most sensible answer. After considering those two possibilities you may still want to (or have to) stay in the situation. Then these techniques are appropriate to reduce your pain and increase your joy.

Get involved with living, go for experiences, that's where learning takes place. Learning inherently feels good. It's nature's way of rewarding us for growing. And if we don't learn, we become dull and boring to others while suffering from boredom and a lack of meaning in our own lives. That's nature's way of saying, "Get with it!"

The acorn already contains what it takes to become an oak tree. You already contain what it takes to become a human being. And by choosing to change the "inner attitudes" of your mind, you can also change the "outer aspects" of your life. You can be a magnificent human being and **feel good**, too!

Section I Stories

These stories involve both clinical and personal experiences. They illustrate one or more of the points or observations which I've made elsewhere. The clinical stories come from my experiences in training, in my work as a counselor on campus, or from my work in private practice. (The names have been changed.) Many of these stories will be referred to in Section II The Big Lie.

The greatest discovery of my generation is that human beings by changing the inner attitudes of their minds can change the outer aspects of their lives. It is too bad that more people will not accept this tremendous discovery and begin living it.

WILLIAM JAMES

Play Ball!

One day I was discussing his career with a young graduate student as he struggled to decide what to do with his life. He was 32 years old. He thought he had decided on his goal, but still wanted to discuss the subject. His goal, his purpose in life, was to become a professional baseball player.

Why did he want to be a pro? So he could have money. Why did he want money? To take care of his family so he would be fulfilling his responsibilities. He wanted to fulfill his responsibilities so that he would feel successful. And why did he want to feel successful? Because he believed that feeling successful would make him **feel good**.

Right there I had an "Aha!" reaction. His real goal was to feel good. What he was calling his "goal" was really the means he had chosen to achieve the end result of feeling good. The end, and the means of achieving that end were being confused. I wondered, "Is everyone's goal or purpose in life to **feel good**?" I knew that I had to do some more thinking on that subject. (Cancel, cancel that last statement. I don't "have to" do anything. I **wanted to** think some more about goals and the purpose in life.)

Anyway, the discussion opened up a much wider range of choices for his life. He was no longer "stuck" with that one goal of being a successful pro baseball player, which was not too likely at his age. There were many career paths which could lead to the desired end. He simply needed to make a realistic choice.

I'm A Failure

George was in his thirties. He said he had been painfully shy all of his life and was darn tired of it. He wanted very much to be more outgoing. He had joined a local fraternal organization in order to have more opportunity to mix socially with others. But just joining the club hadn't done much good, so he had come to see me for some suggestions.

His first assignment was to go walk around the campus that morning and speak to four people. To put some teeth into the project, he agreed that he would not eat lunch until he reported back to me regarding the results of his efforts. (That's Grandma's Law of Behavior Modification--do what you gotta do before you can do what you wanta do.)

At about 11:45 he returned to my office. He looked like an ambulatory case of rejection, discouragement and defeat. His whole appearance, posture and shuffle announced that "I'm a failure."

"What happened?" I asked.

"I did what I was supposed to do, but only one of them answered."

I felt a sudden surge of anger, probably associated with all of the other self-put-downs I'd seen through the years. I slammed my fist down on the desk and yelled at him. "DAMN IT! WHAT WAS YOUR GOAL?"

"Speak to four people."

"AND WHAT DID YOU DO?"

"I spoke to four people . . .Oh, that was **100%, not 25%!**"

It's really much simpler to succeed if your goal is under your control instead of the control of others, even strangers.

14

I Had A Baby Out of Wedlock

When I was in graduate school in the mid-sixties I had the opportunity to work with a local lady, about 36 years of age. She was frightened, guilty and ashamed. She was one of four children. The other three had all been in some kind of "trouble." She was her parents' pride and joy. You know, "Make your parents proud of you." And she had.

What the parents didn't know was that she, too, had been "in trouble." She had sinned. She had "let her folks down." "It would just kill them if they knew how awful I've been." The more they praised her the more guilt and shame she felt. And now she imagined, in terror, that an 18 year old boy would come to her door and say, "Are you my mother?"

She had become pregnant during her senior year in high school, gone to the city to "work," had her baby and gave it up for adoption. In the late 40's, for those who can't remember that far back, having a baby out of wedlock (my, what a terrible word!) was a catastrophe, pre-marital sex was a sin and living together (cohabitation) was against the law. Now she feared that the awful truth would come out.

It struck me that she was condemning herself most severely. I offered an alternate interpretation for her consideration.

"Have you ever known a childless couple who longed for a baby to love and to raise? What a wonderful gift, your own baby, so that he can be loved in a 'legitimate' home. And the couple can choose him as a son, as their very own. Can you imagine what happiness your gift has given to all three of them?"

This new interpretation, this second opinion made sense to her. It "clicked." She made it her own interpretation. She began to **feel good** Two weeks later she came back. She was bubbling. "My friends are asking about the new me. I have so much more energy. I used to be tired by 8:00 PM, now I'm going strong at midnight."

15

My Daughter Isn't Motivated

I received a call from the parent of a student one day. She said her daughter had a problem. The mother wanted it fixed. The problem? Her daughter wasn't "motivated." "Tell me more about it." So she did.

The mother was upset. (I had an idea then who owned the problem.) Her daughter was attending the university at some expense to the parents, who had only limited funds.

But the daughter wouldn't study her chemistry and biology. All she wanted to do was play basketball. They had a backboard and a hoop on the garage. The girl would spend up to six hours a day dribbling and shooting baskets. Not motivated? Really!

The mother wanted a daughter who was a nurse. The daughter wanted to teach physical education and coach girls' basketball. The problem wasn't motivation. It was, "who owns whom?" I was reminded of what Kahlil Gibran said in THE PROPHET:

Your children are not your children. They come through you but not from you. You may give them your love but not your thoughts, for they have their own thoughts.

Don't they, though! To succeed at someone else's goal is to have an empty victory. To deny one's own unique outlet may be hazardous to one's health, as Lawrence LeShan, reporting on the results of his research with cancer patients, states in his book, YOU CAN FIGHT FOR YOUR LIFE.

"....The drive to complete and fulfill himself is seen as existing at the deepest levels of the individual. But for the individual's potential to be realized, there must be an outlet--and it is this outlet that the cancer patient has denied himself in his attempt to gain the love of others by being the person **they** wish him to be."

16

I Was Molested By My Father

A young married student dropped in one day saying that her sex life was not much fun lately. Each time they made love her mind flashed back to when her father had molested her. She felt so much shame that there was very little joy in sex.

The father thought it was his responsibility to teach each of his daughters about sex. He convinced the mother, too. At an appropriate age he took each daughter to the cabin, fondled her and tried to get her to beg him for penetration. She admitted that the fondling was physically enjoyable, it felt good. But mentally she was very ashamed about what was happening. She decided that if something that bad felt good to her, it must mean that she was a bad person. We needed a new interpretation.

The fact that the fondling felt good also meant that her physical body had normal, healthy responses. No, it didn't mean that she was "bad," it meant that she was fortunate. If anyone had a problem, it was her father. This second opinion allowed her to feel good.

Of course not all re-interpretations of past events are that quick and easy. But some of them are. So why not get the easy ones out of the way and move on to bigger challenges?

An Exciting Teacher

She wasn't my teacher but I worked with her at the laboratory school at Winona State University, Winona, Minnesota in 1969. She taught second grade and had been there for years and years. She was in her seventies and we were still getting permission to keep her on the staff. But she was young in heart and mind. She had the energy of a teenager. She literally bounced joyously around the room. It was like magic to watch her with those kids. Also, to watch those kids respond to her!

She had 28 open, honest observers to give her feedback. The last few minutes of the day was a session to increase the awareness of the teacher as well as the kids. While waiting for the school bus, she would ask the children, "What did I do today that helped you learn and grow?" She really wanted answers -- and they gave them to her. She had close to 50 years of experience and was still learning. The kids loved being treated as valuable observers, which they were. Often a child would ask her, "What did I do that made teaching easier or more fun for you?" Then she would increase **their** awareness about being a good student and learner. I think that Kay Dunlay knew the secrets. First, keep learning. If you don't, you'll be both boring and bored. Second, the best learning comes from sharing, not from memorizing. Third, everyone can learn something from anyone. Fourth, caring motivates. And fifth, learning **feels good.**

I Was a High School Drop-out

When I was a teacher/principal in Stromsburg, Nebraska, a fellow teacher confided in me that he was a high school drop-out. I was very surprised because he was a good teacher and a very solid citizen. The theory then was that "drop-outs never amount to anything." That was the "scare" tactic which was being used to keep kids from dropping out. But here he was, amounting to something. Surprise! I had bought into one of the current prejudices. (The scare tactic was used with drugs, too, but it didn't work there either. When I was in junior high, a visiting dignitary, hoping to impress us with the lethal effects of booze, put some whiskey in a glass and dropped a worm in it. The worm died. We learned that if you have worms, you'd better take some booze!) But here was this teacher who had decided to take charge of his life and that's what he did. He went to college without graduating from high school. It was his choice, his goal. He was glad he had done it.

I thought about this "drop-out" 16 years later when I was Superintendent of Schools in Sisters, Oregon. A young man who had just completed four years in the Navy wanted to come to our school and be a "drop-in." The School Board had some concerns about an older man in the midst of those kids. But we decided that we were in the business of education, that the ex-Navy man wanted some, and that we would furnish it. The plan worked out beautifully. The kids who "had to" attend school gave some serious thought to why anyone would come back after they were "free." Until then they had enjoyed the luxury of resisting that which they were compelled to do, without even considering whether or not they would choose to attend, if given a choice.

When you make something "compulsory" you imply that anyone in their right mind wouldn't touch it with a ten-foot pole. That is an awful stigma to put on something which is as rewarding as learning. (Can you remember, for example, the exhilaration you felt when you learned to ride a bicycle?) The compulsory attendance laws have a lot more to do with state financial aid to the school district than with sound principles of learning. If the kids don't attend, the district doesn't get the money. Then the local taxes go up. (Now you're into a serious topic!)

The original intent of compulsory education had nothing to do with compulsory attendance. It was the parents who were "compelled" to allow their children to attend school. It was to prohibit enforced child labor.

I have a hunch that if attendance were not compulsory, we wouldn't need armed guards in the hallways. Then classes would be much more relevant and teachers would make clear the worth of their subject matter. (I remember one day washing my new '71 VW and the thought went through my mind, *"non solum, sed etiam"* or something like that. It was Latin and meant "not only - but also" and was used to tie phrases together. Jocy Carter taught me that in about 1936. It hit me that if I was ever going to find a use for that bit of information, I'd better get with it. Now, at last, after 50 years I've used it as an example of unused learning!) In looking back, I would be willing to trade that bit of Latin for some knowledge about my own human worth; about how to take charge of my feelings (especially fear); the power of beliefs; how to really listen; how to visualize success; how to handle stress; what to do when someone you love is dying; how to feel good without alcohol, drugs, cars, sex or new designer-label clothes; how to find a good mechanic; what happens to an IRA in 30 years; or where to get a good discount.

I Have To Be Tense To Do My Job!

Martha was sent to me for some biofeedback treatments for her tension headaches. Her job was to be "creative," she said, and she "had to be tense in order to be creative." She was a writer. Being an intelligent, conscientious lady, she wanted to do a good job. And, believing that she **had** to be tense to do a good job, she proceeded to be good and tense! Consequently she suffered from headaches. In a strange, self-defeating way the headaches seemed to be evidence that she was diligent and responsible.

During the session she told me about the masterpiece she had completed recently, and how relaxed she had been. Her associates, who were familiar with her job and her work, said that it was the best she had ever done. She agreed. It **was** good.

But Martha was confused. She couldn't believe how easy that project had been. It had just "flowed" effortlessly. She was amazed and a bit confused.

"Martha," I asked, "are you aware that you have been lying to yourself? Earlier you told me that you had to be tense to do your job well, and now you are telling me that the best creative work you ever did was easy and flowed effortlessly."

She was boxed in, between "a rock and a hard place." Her desire to do a good job was the "rock" and her belief that she had to be tense to do a good job was the "hard place."

She didn't need much relaxation training. Once she took charge and questioned her mistaken belief, she was able to relax at work without feeling that she was neglecting her job. Then she could then feel both good and relaxed.

I Killed My Father

Years ago I worked with a very intelligent, 75 year old gentleman using biofeedback. Specifically, he was using the temperature trainer to develop a relaxation skill. Normally at the beginning of a session his finger tip temperature would be about 86 degrees F. In six or eight minutes he could warm it up to about 94 degrees F, a fairly relaxed state for him. One day he came in shuffling his feet, head down, shoulders drooping. His initial temperature was 72. After forty minutes he had warmed up to only 76. "Okay," I said, "What is wrong?" Still looking down at the floor, he monotoned, "Tomorrow is the anniversary of my father's death, and I killed him."

I thought to myself, "Boy, that is heavy!" I said, "It sounds as if you need to talk to your father." He looked up for the first time and said, "Oh Wally, if I only could!"

"You can. Close your eyes. Can you see your father's face? (He nods.) Go ahead, talk to him. I'll answer for your father."

He started immediately, "Dad, please forgive me for marrying a Catholic and causing your heart attack."

"Son, I always wanted you to be your own man...choosing your own wife is a part of that...I forgive you...Please forgive yourself...I know now that I caused my own anger...I caused my own heart attack."

We talked along those lines for fifteen minutes, till the end of the session. Then we noticed that his finger tip temperature had gone up 16 degrees in those 15 minutes. He had relaxed. He was **feeling better.**

That crooked conclusion, that bad interpretation, that "stinking thinking" had been arrived at and stored in words such as these: "If I hadn't married a Catholic, my father would not have had a heart attack and he would still be alive. Therefore, I killed my father." That was the thinking of a distraught young man. Almost everyone knows that marrying a Catholic is not murder!

(Many people have married Catholics and really enjoyed it.) But this very intelligent man had not had the opportunity to give himself a second opinion. Each time he was reminded of those events, he became emotionally distraught again and was unable to think clearly.

We each can take charge and allow ourselves a "second opinion" on all of the traumatic events in our past. With a new, more realistic interpretation we could fix our own feelings.

That was the day I really learned that the mind, through words, and the body are very much connected; that unfinished emotional business carries with it enough power to literally tie a man's body in knots 45 years later; and that those knots may sometimes be untied in just a few minutes by discharging those old emotions.

As he was leaving the office he said, "I wish Dad had been here today." "How do you know he wasn't?" I asked. He looked thoughtful for a moment and said, "I think he was." It was a good day, a day to remember.

I Was Lucky

Many people believe that the past can't be changed. Baloney! It's true that you can't undo past events, but it isn't the **event** that gives me the emotional meaning of the past, it is my current **interpretation** of the event. It's the interpretation that gives me the feeling. It is **my** interpretation and I can re-interpret the event if I choose to do so.

I met a man once who, as a child, was bounced from one foster home to another. A likely interpretation would have been, "What a lousy deal! Nobody cares about me. I'll never have a chance. I can't possibly amount to anything. It will always be this way. It isn't fair!"

But instead he told me, "I was lucky. I watched six mothers and six fathers--close up. I **know** about parenting. I know how to be a good father, and I know a good mother when I meet one. I have a terrific advantage over most people."

This man may have wallowed in self pity for years. I don't know at what age he settled on this interpretation, but there was certainly no need to change it now. He was already **feeling good.** He had taken what would normally be seen as a less than desirable childhood and made it into a good experience. His feelings didn't need fixing.

I Can't Stand It!

I remember a lady I talked to once in a counseling session. She came in really steaming. "I can't stand that crabby old SOB another minute! For 32 years it's been the same old story. He's always telling me everything I do wrong. He even goes back to when we were dating to criticize me!"

Appropriate or not, I laughed out loud. Something about having 32 years of experience with the same event and still being bugged by it struck me as funny. (She didn't hit me so we went on.) She already had herself "programmed" to be unable to stand it. And being upset left her creative problem solving ability at zero.

I explained that it sounded as if her husband had always been critical; that he was probably unhappy with himself, too; that he needed to "vomit" his unhappiness periodically; but she need **not** stand in the line-of-fire. It wasn't meant for her. Just interpret his emotional upset as if it were a stomach upset. Remember, he very much needs to vomit that poisonous feeling. Don't say to yourself, "I can't stand it." That is a lie because you have been standing it for 32 years. Just say to yourself, "That's interesting. He's been that way ever since I met him. He'll probably be that way again. It's good for him to puke it up. His upset in no way diminishes me."

We spent an hour and a half together. As she left she paused at the door, grinned sheepishly and said, "I can hardly wait to try it out!" She had changed her inner attitude. She had some new words to say to herself. She felt good. She was taking charge. She **could** stand it, maybe for another 32 years.

If I Could Just Make Him Understand

One lady I worked with had been contemplating divorce for several years. Her husband seemed to be quite insensitive to any of her needs. For several years she had used wooden boxes for end tables. She had no furniture in which to store her clothes. And there had been no door on the bathroom for about three years. Repeated discussions had changed nothing.

It wasn't that they were poor. She had a good income, as did he. But all of the spare money went for **his** hobby, breeding and raising thoroughbred animals.

She had given up trying and filed for divorce. Somehow, she felt that she couldn't leave him until he understood **why** she wanted a divorce. All he had to do was say, "I just don't understand it," and she was blocked.

When she realized that she would probably never be able to make him understand and, in fact, had no obligation to, she felt a tremendous relief. She finally realized that her need to make him understand gave him veto power over her. She then took charge and took back her power.

There's Nothing I Can Do!

You're a parent. Your adolescent son or daughter is out of control, on drugs, a run-away, or in trouble with the authorities. You've done everything you can and still you worry and fret and toss and turn through those sleepless nights. Those are not very satisfying solutions to your feelings of helplessness. In fact they are detrimental to yourself, your child and to the emotional environment.

If you are a psychologist and parents come to you with such a frustration, you may find that the "helpless" feeling they have is contagious and you can catch it right quick! There just has to be something that could help. The parents wanted to do **something** and I wanted a positive suggestion to offer them. Then I thought of a possibility. In my search for pieces to the "cosmic jigsaw puzzle" I had read MASTER GUIDE TO PSYCHISM by Harriet Boswell. In this book she had described how some psychics try to protect themselves from negative energy systems or spirits. (The theory is that energy systems cannot be destroyed. If you have the energy system of an SOB and you die, you are free on the other side with that same basic personality. That makes me wonder about capital punishment!) Anyway, Boswell says that psychics should use their consciousness to create an imaginary "bubble" of white light or love around themselves before venturing off into that unknown space. This bubble of love serves as a protective armor to fend off negative vibrations and spirits.

Maybe this was the idea for which I was searching. But it looked like quite a task. Here we have a parent (usually one, sometimes two) who is "broadcasting" a huge program of fear and worry vibes and he/she is supposed to switch suddenly to broadcasting love and light! But if Marcus Aurelius and William James are right, then it can be done.

But how? I've observed that it is almost impossible to recall a happy memory when everything is going wrong. It's as if we have one file drawer for all of the awful feelings and we can't even remember that there is another drawer in the feeling file cabinet which contains good feelings. Getting out of the muck and mire of the bad feelings drawer takes some doing. With a mother, especially, I often ask, "Do you remember the very first time you saw that child?" Then I ask that they tell me about it. Soon they are in touch with some tender, loving memories. "Tell me about all of the fun times, and as you do, feel that warm glow develop around your heart area. You may want to imagine that the sun is beaming a column of light straight down on your head and adding to the warmth in your heart area. Now when you feel an overflowing of the love and light, aim a beam of it to your child, wherever he/she might be. Know that the beam will travel straight from your heart and find him/her."

I have suggested the use of the bubble of light to persons other than parents, too. One young man was so angry with his sister from New York when she visited him in Minnesota for Christmas that he got out of **his** car and walked home in a snow storm. Now that is being ticked off! They had fought as children and still had unfinished business. He practiced the "light" meditation daily for a couple of weeks. He said he didn't know if it helped her but it certainly helped him. (She wrote a letter making peace a few weeks later.)

Another opportunity to suggest the use of light presented itself one day when a dentist came to my office. He was very tense. His business was going great but he could not stand much more of the stress and strain. I thought of Boswell's bubble of light. I'm sure that the concept was outside the reality box of the dentist, but he didn't laugh. He was quite desperate. What did he have to lose? I explained that we are surrounded by an energy field and that the nature of that field seems to depend on our emotional state at that time. I also explained that the energy fields of his patients could be affecting his field and his emotions, thus producing tension in him.

Now if you have about four little offices up and down the hall and each of the offices has a dental chair containing one very frightened and hurting patient, you have an emotional en-

vironment that calls for some protection from all of those negative vibrations. So I suggested that before he started his day
he could spend a few minutes in private meditation, using
memories which would give rise to that feeling of warmth from
which he could mentally create his protective bubble of light.

In three weeks this quiet, reserved man came bouncing in
saying, "Wally it was just **fantastic!** I've never had such relaxed
patients. It worked so well for me that I started to make my
bubble big enough to contain my patients also. Then I asked
one of my assistants (the open-minded one) to add to the bubble
when she was doing routine work and was mentally free to do
so." That was another good day.

I'm a Good Coach / I'm a Bad Coach

I was doing a workshop in Iowa a few years ago for a group of teachers. The topic was human relations. I had included relationship with one's self, which seemed natural, since the self is human, too. I wanted to emphasize what happens to us when we say bad things about ourselves. Bad-mouthing is what I call it. I asked for a volunteer for this demonstration.

The wrestling coach from one of the local high schools stepped forward. He was a big, and I mean BIG man. Built like a brick outhouse (paraphrased) as they say in those parts.

First I asked him to stick out his left arm and lock it in place. I tried to pull it down, but no luck. I had him put his arm down and instructed him to repeat, over and over, one of two thoughts. He was to repeat to himself either, "I'm a good coach, I'm a good coach" or "I'm a bad coach, I'm a bad coach." When one of those thoughts was firmly planted in his mind he was to raise his arm as before and I would test his strength. Then I would test him with the other thought and tell him which thought was in his mind on each test.

He took a moment, then raised his arm. It was like a rock. I tried both of my hands. Still locked. He put his arm down, took a few moments to plant the other thought in his mind, then raised it when he was ready. I pulled, the arm collapsed. His eyes bugged out in total surprise. I suggested that he apologize to his body for investing his mental energy in such a negative statement. Words and thoughts have awesome powers. Take charge of your mind! (John Diamond, MD, talks about kinesiology in his two books, LIFE FORCE and YOUR BODY DOESN'T LIE.)

We Screwed Up, Sir!

It was 1959 at Mountain Home Air Force Base in Idaho, just before I became a civilian again. Each afternoon at 1600 hours (that's 4:00 in the afternoon for most people) a Commander's Briefing was scheduled. All the units were represented: maintenance, armament, electronics, operations, radar, refueling, the bomber squadrons, etc. The agenda was to critique yesterday's training and to brief tomorrow's missions. Often it amounted to fixing responsibility and blame. Many invisible shields were in place with fingers "at the ready" to point to another organization.

Something had gone wrong yesterday. The bombers and the tankers had not met at the rendezvous point at the right time. Several training missions had not gone as planned. There was a serious error, but who was to blame?

"What happened?" asked General Kingsbury. Silence, the dread silence of apprehension. Then Bill Becklund, Commander of the Air Refueling Squadron, sounded off. "We screwed up, Sir." Now there was more silence. This time it was a stunned, surprised silence. After a long pause the General said, "OK, Bill. Don't let it happen again."

I had always liked Bill and appreciated the way he ran his squadron. That day I admired him as a person. It wasn't just that he took responsibility, but he claimed it with dignity. He was in charge. I was obviously impressed, or I wouldn't be remembering the incident in 1986.

I had hoped to see Bill at the 9th Bomb Wing reunion in Boise last June and thank him for that experience, but he wasn't there. If you know Bill, please pass the word along for me.

A Student Pilot's Second Opinion

The year is 1944, it is late evening and I'm flying as an instructor with a student in a B-25. We are in the San Antonio area. So are a lot of others. Several planes are using the radio range to practice instrument flying techniques. The air is full of radio calls, lots of chatter, position reports, etc. The planes are all capable of talking to the outside world by pushing the microphone button forward with the thumb while still holding the control wheel firmly and using the throat mike pressed tightly against the Adam's apple. Pulling the mike button backward allows one to speak only to those on that airplane.

If you have ever tried to fly a new plane in a new area on a new radio range, you know that you can get very busy. Your hands are busy on the controls trying to maintain a heading, altitude and airspeed. The feet are busy with the rudders trying to make coordinated turns. You are adjusting the power, talking on the radio and trying to get a mental picture from the radio range signals in your ear. Are you in an "A" quadrant or an "N" quadrant? Inbound or outbound? It can become frustrating. Apparently, it was too frustrating for this student. The chatter was normal and then, suddenly this loud voice came on the air, full of frustration and just dripping with disgust. "Aw sh--! I'm all f---ed up!" SILENCE. Nobody said a word. Dozens of pilots smiled in the dark, recognizing the situation. They had all been there. The tower at north Alamo field broke the silence after a few moments. "Will the aircraft which made that last transmission please give me your identification number." Those moments must have felt like an eternity to the young man who pushed his thumb the wrong way on his microphone button and said to the whole world what he had intended for the privacy of interphone. In those moments he had a brief opportunity to reach a "second opinion" regarding the evaluation of his condition. Then the student pilot broke the silence. In calm, measured tones he stated with much dignity, "I'm not **that** f---ed up."

In a brief, thought-filled moment he had changed his feeling state from one catastrophe to one of inconvenience. As I recall, the rest of the evening was uneventful, at least by comparison.

I'm Shaking All Over and It Isn't Even Cold

I think I must have been born afraid. My earliest memory involved fear. I lived on a farm and only saw civilization on some Saturdays when I sat in the back of the Model T in Orchard, Nebraska by McBride's store. Mahood's Ford garage was two blocks west on the other side of the street. That was the Orchard business district. To the north a block or two was a little white wooden church. That's the scene of my earliest memory. It was Sunday, February 13, 1924, my third birthday. The kids had to go up front and put a penny in that heavy white coffee cup to "celebrate" being a year older. I was afraid, but I got pushed into it anyway.

My next memory of fear was when I was in kindergarten. I lived in three houses and went to two schools in that year, another house and another school in first grade. By the first day of school in the second grade I had lived in five houses (besides the farm each summer) and attended four schools. I was scared to death most of the time. It was at the second house my kindergarten year that I was really frightened. It was evening, already dark. The home on the other side of the driveway was on fire. I'd never heard a siren or seen a firetruck flashing its lights. The air was electric with emotion. I was terrorized and trembling uncontrollably. I said out loud to nobody in particular, "I'm shaking all over and it isn't even cold." That seemed to be funny to everyone else. They laughed. It became a family joke. Not funny. I had trouble dealing with fear for the next 40 years. I had been ridiculed for being fearful. After that I wouldn't admit to feeling fear. I resisted doing anything I perceived as frightening. Nobody could understand my resistance. Grandma said I was the most stubborn child she had ever seen. (I thought, "It takes one to know one!") Nobody knew I was afraid, but they knew I resisted going out at 4:30 AM on a scary country road to deliver newspapers.

Let's Choose Up Sides

At recess time on the playground of Riley grade school in Lincoln, Nebraska, a suggestion such as that would strike terror in my heart, produce an empty, sinking feeling in my gut and a looseness in the bowels. Oh, for a hole in the ground to crawl into. The best two baseball players are the team captains. They do the choosing of their teams. It's not the Miss America contest. That is judging between winners and near-winners. This is selection of the worst, the one most likely to strike out, the one who can't hit the ball for sour owl dung. And I'm either last or next to it. Boy, it takes a long time to finish the choosing process. Then if the team which got "stuck" with me groaned, that didn't make my day.

So I avoided the pain of baseball for those years, and consequently got worse and worse as a batter.

I wish I had known then that my worth as a human being did not depend on my performance on the playground. I'm glad that I understand it today. Even now if I pass a playground and see that selection process going on, I feel for the one who is going to be chosen last. I am **not** my performance, I am the **performer**. My worth as a human being is never in question. That worth is a gift, just because I **am** human. Never again will I give any person or any organization the power to evaluate and set my worth as a human being. It is just too devastating. Besides, that's another inside job, and I'm in charge of it.

Take Off That Sweater!

Many of us really believe that our feelings are caused by the behavior of others. This is not true. But we cling to that false belief, proving that we are right by saying that, "If you hadn't done that, I wouldn't feel this way."

There is a grand lady in Nebraska who gave me the greatest illustration of this error in placing blame.

Years ago we were visiting her home. It was spring, a nice, cool day. Her husband, who had a bad heart and poor circulation, was wearing a brown sweater. She, being somewhat overweight, did not feel cool at all. I was amazed when she looked across the living room at him and said, with much authority and conviction, **"Raymond, take off that sweater! You look so hot I just can't stand it!"**

It seemed so natural to her that the discomfort which she felt was caused by his wearing of the sweater.

The problem with this way of viewing the cause of our feelings is that we can't get comfortable until we can get the other person to change what he or she is doing. If we can convince others that they really are the cause of our feelings, then **they** will feel guilty and uncomfortable. Then they may stop what they are doing in order to relieve their own guilt. But changing their behavior to make others comfortable could make them resentful.

Believing this lie, that my feelings are caused by your behavior, is at the core of most human relations problems. It sounds so simple to overcome, but it's not easy. Our language habit keeps us brainwashed into believing that others are the problem. As Pogo used to say, "We have met the enemy and they is us."

Don't Tell Him He's Dying

I arrived home from the Pensacola Naval Air Station on September 3, 1943. Pop was very ill. At that time Hodgkin's Disease was incurable with a life expectancy of one or two years from the time of discovery of the first swollen lymph node. His time was about to run out. When I went in to see him I was told that the doctor had ordered that Pop not be told that he was dying. He might give up hope. (That's hope which the same doctor said didn't exist. The deception had started.)

I sat on the edge of the bed. He was conscious and recognized me. In a few minutes he got right to the topic which was on his mind. He said, "Wallace, they are giving me medicine to regulate my heart and they are giving me medicine to kill the pain; but they are not giving me anything to make me well." He was ready to talk. He wanted to talk about it. He needed to talk about it. I wasn't going to lie for that doctor, but I didn't have the guts to defy him and maybe all nine of my siblings. So I just sat there and looked out the window. In the evening nine days later, several family members were gathered at the foot of his bed. He came to momentarily and asked, "What are we waiting for?" He died about 6:30 the next morning without talking to anyone about his apprehensions, or the trip he was going to take. He died without saying even a single "goodbye."

It was the most cruel form of isolation at a time when togetherness was most appropriate. I think it was the doctor who needed to deny reality, but it was Mom and the family who paid the price for that denial. But those were the days when the doctor was the boss. "Doctor knows best" was one of the sayings. Good people didn't question the authorities, they just followed orders--and lived with the consequences.

Now we tend to hire the doctor as a consultant, consider the advice but make our own decisions. That's taking charge.

If a doctor today suggested injecting deceit and dishonesty into a family system, he should and probably would be dismissed. Now we know that the richest and most meaningful communication can take place in those final days, hours and even minutes. Don't allow yourself to be cheated out of that time.

I Loved Him Too Much

When Mike, our fifth child, was about five years old we were living in Bend, Oregon. Mike was a curious little boy. I say "was" because Mike isn't with us any longer. He became a South Dakota statistic on March 24, 1965. He was a traffic fatality that year, number 44. (It isn't difficult to remember dates when there is emotion attached.)

Mike was curious, always absorbed in something. On this day in Bend he had found a tiny frog. He carried it around with him all afternoon. He really liked it. Later he brought it to his mother to show her. He opened his little hand. The frog didn't move. "He's dead," Mike said. "But I wanted him to live, Mommy. I guess I loved him too much."

No, Mike didn't love the frog too much. But he did hold him too tightly. Holding too tightly can be disastrous to a loving relationship; it can smother it.

I'll Never Forget Those Storm Windows

We were enclosing the breezeway of our home in Winona, Minnesota. We had already carpeted the floor and added solid doors. It still wasn't warm enough so we decided to put up storm windows. The cabinet shop had made one large wooden storm window to cover each pair of windows. That was a little better, but we still needed more protection from that Minnesota cold.

So, Saturday morning we were putting plastic over the storm windows. I had done a real good job. I'd put strips across and up and down. Each window had about 16 sections to it. I had just finished tacking the last strip in place. With one tack every four inches, there were a lot of tacks! My wife and I were going to put the window in place, then have lunch. As we picked it up I noticed that the spring-loaded pins were between the glass and the plastic and could not be retracted for the window to go into place. I had placed the plastic on the wrong side of the window!

I could feel the anger start to boil. Words like "darn it" and "oh shucks" came to my mind. Not exactly those words, but similar ones. Thoughts like, "Why does this have to happen to me?" and "It isn't fair!" The anger was right there, just ready to pump adrenalin into my system.

I had been teaching Dr. Albert Ellis' Rational Emotive therapy in a class just that week so his ideas were fresh in my mind. I remembered to say, "It isn't a catastrophe, it's just an inconvenience." I took charge of my self-talk just in the nick of time. The anger didn't materialize. We had lunch. Then I did it right. It was an "aha!" for me. This stuff really works. It felt good, knowing how to stop creating anger.

Mom's Insights

Mom died on February 12, 1986, just six months ago. She spent her last year and a half in our home. She would have been 96 on March I. Her mental retrieval system didn't work too well at the end. When I was young we would have said that "she'd lost her marbles," or "she wasn't playing with a full deck," or "she didn't have a full set of dishes." I'm 65 now so I don't talk that way so much.

She spent a lot of time "floating around" the universe. Technically, it would probably be called hallucinating. (I find it interesting that the people who don't see the "things" or hear the "voices" are the ones who get to define what they have neither seen nor heard!) Mom also spent a lot of time wrestling with the events surrounding her sister's wedding. There was a lot of conflict then and she was still working it out more than 70 years later.

My dad was more fundamental in his religion than my mother or her family. Mom felt that her brothers and sisters had rejected her after she got married in 1912. One day she said, "Daddy was more strict than my family. I had always thought that they were rejecting me, but I guess I had moved away from **them**."

Mom was a "soft-sell" Christian. But she firmly believed that it was her job to try and get people to be more Christ-like. One day she commented that she used to think it was her job to change people, but now she thought it was her job just to love them and let them change when they were ready.

I usually checked her mental state in the morning. "Who are you?" If she was really sharp that day she would say, "Charlotte Berry Johnston." Then I'd ask, "And who am I?" On a good day she'd say "William Wallace Johnston," or "Wally." If she got that far I would ask her, "And what is our relationship?" Sometimes I was her father, sometimes a brother or an uncle. It was a real struggle for her to recall our relationship. One morning when I

41

went through the routine she got my name right, but said that I was her uncle. Later in the day we had visitors and I reported on her performance, adding that I had given her a B for the day. She was miffed about the grade and a bit testy. The last time I went through the routine she was correct on my name, couldn't recall her name, and when I asked about our relationship, she said very crisply, "I don't think that matters as long as there is love." I didn't quiz her after that.

People are amazing creatures. To watch Mom struggle to get rid of the old conflict, to understand what had happened, and to get new insights was a special privilege. The satisfaction from learning can last right up to the very end of life. That's encouraging. It's never too late to take charge and work out your feelings and have new insights.

Section II The Big Lie

Because I see this misconception as **THE** major problem in human relationships, I have chosen to make a separate section to deal with it. When we are **wrong** in determining the **cause** of our feelings, then we **attack, blame,** or **manipulate** the **wrong source**. This solves nothing, and causes much resentment.

In this section I will refer back to some of the stories which illustrate this erroneous belief about the cause of our feelings, and describe some solutions for the problem.

The Big Lie:
You Are Responsible For My Feelings

"Take off that sweater, you look so hot I just can't stand it!"

"You make me angry."

"You made my day!"

"You made me love you, I didn't want to do it, I didn't want to do it."

"You hurt my feelings."

"You make me very happy."

We tend to talk that way. It's a habit and that habit causes lots of problems. I get to believing that you really **do** cause my feelings. Then I blame you. And the only way I can get any control over my feelings is to get some control over **you**. About the only way I can control you is to make you feel responsible and guilty for causing my discomfort. Then to get rid of your guilt you have to stop doing whatever you were doing and do something that meets my approval. Naturally that causes re-

* * * * *

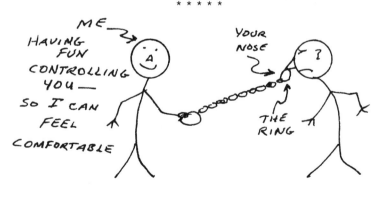

* * * * *

sentment in you. So I get rid of my discomfort by causing guilt in you. You get rid of the guilt by changing, but that causes resentment in you. As long as I can keep you believing that you caused my feelings, then I "gotcha." It's like I have a ring in your nose and I can pull you around with your guilt. This is not a good technique for creating more joy and less pain. Quite the opposite. Besides, it's a BIG LIE. I am responsible for my own feelings.

It isn't the event out there in the world or what you are doing that is upsetting me. That is only the trigger, not the cause. The "bullet" that I hurt myself with is the mental activity in my head. It's the thinking, the believing, the assuming, concluding, judging, expecting, and the interpreting; all of the mental activity. This mental activity determines the meaning of the event for me. And there is always a feeling with a meaning. Without feelings, an item is "meaningless." The meaning is the "bullet" which wounds us. Self-inflicted pain is an inside job.

* * * * *

MENTAL ACTIVITY DETERMINES THE MEANING OF THE EVENT.

THE MEANING IS THE "BULLET" WHICH WOUNDS ME.

MY PERCEPTION THE "TRIGGER"

AN EVENT WHICH OCCURS IN THE WORLD

I BELIEVE THE EVENT CAUSES THE PAIN.

NOT TRUE!

* * * * *

To keep from being wounded we must either eliminate the trigger or the bullet. Since eliminating the trigger involves trying to control and manipulate you as well as trying to control all of the events in my world, it seems advisable to concentrate on controlling the mental activity in my own head, the "bullet." That will allow you to do your thing and the world can proceed on its way without me at the helm. What a relief! Controlling my whole world and the people in it was a big job. No wonder I've been tired.

So the bad news is that I have to stop blaming you for my

feelings. The good news is that I can control my feelings myself, if I can learn how! Here are some suggestions. They are simple, but you have to be alert.

First, be alert about the way you talk, because the big lie is embodied in language. You need to learn to talk differently, or you are constantly brain-washing yourself into believing the lie by your word habits. That has already been mentioned.

Second, train yourself to tune in to what's going on in your visceral area, the "gut." When some feelings start rumbling around down there, ask for time out, hold up your hand, take time to ask yourself, "What am I feeling?"

After identifying the feeling, start searching for the mental activity which caused that feeling. Was it what you thought, told yourself, remembered, assumed, concluded, judged, or the way in which you interpreted the triggering event that created the meaning for you? The feeling you have will give you a hint or a clue about your mental activity. Do you feel hurt, rejected, diminished, left out, insulted, ignored, violated, stupid, embarrassed?

When you have identified the feeling start searching for the meaning which is tied to it. What did that event **mean**? That I'm not OK, that they don't love me, that I'm unlovable, that I have failed, that I **am** a failure, that I goofed, that I don't count, that I'm not acceptable, that I'm worth-less?

When you are aware of some such meaning, say, "Cancel-cancel that interpretation." Just to be sure, mentally write down that interpretation on an imaginary piece of paper and throw it into an imaginary bonfire.

Now, having identified the feeling, the mental activity which caused it and the meaning which served as the "bullet" to wound yourself, it's time to reverse the process. So find a positive interpretation, a second opinion, an alternate way of looking at the event. You'll probably find that most of the painful interpretations have to do with you or your behavior being "not-OK." Here it helps to know that "God don't make junk," and to remember Eleanor Roosevelt's insight that "Nobody can make you feel inferior without your permission." Don't give it!

There can be many interpretations of a situation. Suppose

your husband sends you flowers. Does it mean he loves you, or he's relieving his guilt, or he's amorous and preparing you for tonight, or he's having an affair, or he's finally learning to be sensitive and tender?

If your wife bakes your favorite pie, does it mean that she scratched the car, is overdrawn at the bank, bought a new dress, having an affair, or that she finally realizes what a great guy you are?

So pick an interpretation that leaves you feeling calm and positive. If you can't think of any interpretation, you can always say to yourself, "That's interesting, I wonder what it (the event) means."

Now that you have taken time out to identify what you were feeling, found the bad interpretation, destroyed it and created an acceptable interpretation, it is time to reward yourself for your desired behavior. So, physically pat yourself on the back. Yes, get your body into this bit of self-approval. Say, "Nice going, you did it again, I'm proud of you!" Then grin all over and feel good. If people look at you as if you're weird, just smile.

* * * * *

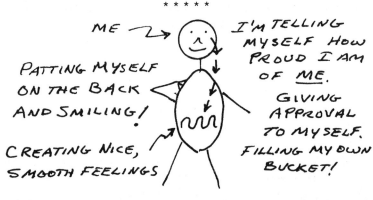

ME ⟶

PATTING MYSELF ON THE BACK AND SMILING!

CREATING NICE, SMOOTH FEELINGS

I'M TELLING MYSELF HOW PROUD I AM OF ME.

GIVING APPROVAL TO MYSELF. FILLING MY OWN BUCKET!

* * * * *

Remember that you are not weird just because others think you are. You are very unusual and very special and you are taking control of your life.

"Ah," you say, "it's just a mind game." (Sec. III) Well of course! But play it to feel good. Be aware. **Know** what you are doing to yourself. Choose good meanings, or neutral ones.

48

Create good vibes, improve the emotional environment of your neighborhood. Now you know what John Milton, Shakespeare, Epictetus, Marcus Aurelius and Alfred Adler were talking about. Give up blaming others, or the world. **Grow up**! Be responsible for yourself. **Happiness is an inside job!** Take charge and change those feelings.

You may not want to be responsible for your own feelings. But the consequences are automatic. Other people will control your emotions as long as you believe the BIG LIE, that your feelings are created by people and events outside your skin and are somehow injected into your gut.

OK, so you're not quite convinced. I'll try to help your disbelief. I don't think you really want to be a "victim" of the events of the world. I don't think you want to have to manipulate and control your friends and relatives through guilt just so you can be more comfortable. (If you **do** want that, it's easy.)

If you read "Beliefs and Their Incredible Power" (Sec. III), it seems certain that the activities of the mind **do** affect the body. "I'm a Good Coach/I'm a Bad Coach" (Sec. I) illustrates how words can reduce one's strength, even if those words are not believed. You may not want to believe these reports, they may be beyond your giggle point or outside your reality box. You may want to say, "It can't be." But remember, in order to know that it can't be, you have to know everything in the universe. (If you're that smart, why the heck are you reading this book?)

Can you remember going to a meeting or a party where something happened but you weren't upset about it at the time? Then driving home you thought about it--and got really ticked off! Well, you were deciding the meaning of the event on the way home. When the bullet, the "felt meaning," hit your gut, "bingo!" It wasn't the event, it was the meaning you chose sometime later.

Did you ever **imagine** that something happened and then you got a big emotional reaction? It couldn't have been the **event** that upset you because there was **no event**. It was your **interpretation** of the "event," the non-happening, which upset you.

Let's look at what upset some of the people in the stories.

In "I Was Molested by My Father" (Sec. I), the lady **concluded** that she was a bad person and **believed** that she should feel ashamed. So she felt rotten. But when she decided that the fact that his fondling felt good **meant** that she had a normal, healthy body, then she felt great.

When I had the problem with the storm windows (Sec. I), all it took was a quick change in self-talk before the anger even materialized, and I aborted the upset.

George, in "I'm a Failure" (Sec. I), spoke to four people and only one of them answered. He interpreted his project as only 25% successful and **decided** that he was a failure. He felt depressed and defeated. Then he realized that his goal was to speak to four people. That is what he did. His second interpretation, which was correct, was that he had completed 100% of his goal and therefore was successful. He felt good.

In "Mom's Insights" (Sec. I), she decided that her brothers and sisters were not rejecting her when she married my dad. She realized 74 years later that **she** had actually moved away from **them**. This new interpretation provided a release from some very old unfinished emotional business.

Martha, in "I Have To Be Tense To Do My Job" (Sec. I), **believed** that tension was a requirement in order to conscientiously do her job. Result? Tension headaches. When she realized that her very best work had been accomplished in an incredibly relaxed state, then she could change her belief and give up her tension headaches.

The lady in "I Had a Baby Out of Wedlock" (Sec. I) felt guilty for 18 years until she realized that giving up her baby boy had probably brought a lot of joy to a previously childless couple. Her new interpretation gave her a good feeling, more energy and a new lease on life.

The "I Was Lucky" case (Sec. I) felt good. He already had a good interpretation. And the woman who had 32 years experience with the critical SOB ("I Can't Stand It," Sec. I) quit the "I can't stand it" self-talk and was looking forward to her next opportunity to handle his criticism in a new way.

The 75 year old gentleman in "I Killed My Father" (Sec. I) reasoned that the event in the world, his marrying a Catholic, actually caused his father's heart attack. He felt responsible for that event, therefore he killed Dad. He could have not married, or married a Methodist, or coerced his fiancee into changing her religion. Then Dad wouldn't have gotten so angry that he had a heart attack. Dad would still be alive. This man believed the BIG LIE, that he was responsible for his father's anger. The belief, "I killed my father," and the meaning, "I am guilty," produced a massive load of guilt which restricted his circulation, literally tying his body in knots 45 years later. After he expressed his guilt, asked for forgiveness and received it, he then relaxed. His hands warmed up rapidly as he realized that his father caused his own anger and heart attack. He gave up the big lie. He felt relieved. He got a reprieve from his own conviction, and was no longer guilty.

Now, if you are convinced, if your clicker has clicked, you'll probably want to take charge of your own feelings. But just ten minutes after your decision to give up the big lie you may hear yourself saying, "You make me angry." Again you have a choice. You can decide that you're a failure and feel lousy. Or you can say, "This is interesting. I'm pleased that I noticed my self-talk habit. That's good awareness. Now I have something with which to work." If you did choose the "failure" interpretation, you can "cancel-cancel," substitute a positive interpretation, pat yourself on the back, say "Nice going, I'm proud of you," and smile.

Feel good each time you catch yourself and reverse the habit. Change your language habit, too. Say things like, "I'm upsetting myself. Give me a moment to get back on track." Then straighten out your mental activity, pat and smile. People may think you're strange, but they'll find you interesting. Remember, their thinking you are weird doesn't make you weird. You know that you have never been more sane in your whole life. That should feel good. You'll also get an immediate pay-off from the self-approving pat on the back.

While some will find you interesting, others may find you hard to deal with. **You** won't be responsible for **their** feelings. You won't have the guilt ring in your nose. They won't be able to lead you around. They'll probably resent the change in you. You have become "unreliable," meaning unpredictable. They invested a lot of energy in learning how to handle you. Now you're different. The change in you has wiped out their investment. They have to start over. You're a new person, a stranger to them. They may even try to make you feel guilty for changing and causing them all that frustration. But you know how to handle that. Be aware. Practice, practice, and enjoy doing it. Pat yourself on the back. Don't predict that "people will think I'm crazy." That mental activity will create embarrassment and you'll stop the process in order to escape the embarrassment which you created. Try "cancel-cancel," compliment yourself and smile. You're not going crazy, you're going **sane**.

Section III Essays

In this section I've written about topics which I think are important to society and which are interesting to me. This is a collection of ideas, opinions, hopes, beliefs, biases and convictions which seem to synthesize what I've learned from my years of living and my 20 years of work as a counseling psychologist.

I have felt free to write what I please. I trust you'll be equally free to accept or reject what you read. I think we can agree to disagree without being disagreeable. Even when you are not in agreement, I hope that your thinking will be stimulated.

On Mind Games

"Ah," you say, "you're just playing mind games when you play around with the interpretation of past events." Well of course! It just might be that **mind games** are the only games in town. If the words create the meaning, and the meaning creates the feeling and the feeling is what gives me the significance and the mind is what handles the words, then of course it is a MIND GAME! But it is an important mind game because it deals with my goals and my purpose in life. The crucial question is this, "Am I playing to win or to lose? Am I playing to feel good, or to feel miserable?"

These mind games include a lot of activities, all of which use words. I use words for my THINKING, for my INTERPRETATIONS, for my BELIEFS, for my ASSUMPTIONS, for my JUDGMENTS, for my EXPECTATIONS, for my CONCLUSIONS, for my SELF-TALK, for the LABELS I hang on myself and others. All of this MENTAL ACTIVITY comes in WORDS. And the words create the meaning for me. And the meaning carries the feelings. And the feelings determine the quality of my life.

Oh, but this is Pollyanna-ish! But Pollyanna changed people with her optimistic attitude. Maybe this approach is more akin to Abe Lincoln's insight that "A man can be about as happy as he decides to be". Is it this MIND GAME that these guys had in mind when they said:

> The mind is its own place, and in itself can make a heaven of hell, and a hell of heaven.
>
> *John Milton*

> Men are not worried by things, but by their ideas about things.
>
> *Epictetus*

> I saw that all things I feared, and which feared me, had nothing good or bad in them save insofar as the mind was affected by them.
>
> *Spinoza*

We are influenced not by "facts" but by our interpretation of facts.
Alfred Adler

There is nothing either good or bad but thinking makes it so.
Shakespeare

If you are pained by an external thing, it is not this thing that disturbs you, but your judgment about it. And it is in your power to wipe out this judgment now.
Marcus Aurelius

Do I really live in the "real world" out there, or do I live in a sea of my own mental activities--the thinking, the judgments, conclusions, expectations, beliefs, assumptions, labels, self-talk and interpretations? If I do live in a sea of mental activity, I'd best be careful not to pollute my own environment with "stinking thinking." Because I'll pay the price in a very reduced quality of life.

I believe I can choose my mental activities. I can take charge. If I choose to believe I have no choice then I am help-less. I predicted correctly! This is tricky because I might want very much to be right. Then I could **feel good** about being **right** about my own helplessness!

Within the province of the mind, what I believe to be true is true or becomes true within the limits to be found experientially and experimentally. These limits are further beliefs to be transcended.
John C. Lilly, MD, in THE CENTER OF THE CYCLONE

My Responsibility

In "The Big Lie" (Sec. II) I talked about my not being responsible for you and your feelings. If I were responsible for you, for whom would you be responsible? I would have "stolen" your responsibility, leaving you non-responsible. And I would have placed a burden on me. I'd feel like a thief, a tired thief.

* * * * *

* * * * *

It seems to be in our nature to want to avoid responsibility. In "Spit Out the Apple" (this section), Adam blamed Eve and Eve blamed the serpent. It goes back a long way. But it is refreshing and memorable when a person does accept responsibility, as Bill did in "We Screwed Up, Sir" (Sec. I). You know then that you are in the presence of maturity.

The argument about who is responsible for whom is pervasive. That's what the heredity/environment argument is about; or the difference between an acorn and a Chevrolet. If I assume that I grow from the inside out, I'm responsible. If society molds me from the outside in, then society is responsible.

Even the way we talk carries a hint of our belief system in it. If asked where they came from, some people would say, "I was born and raised in Slippery Rock." It is implied that from about birth to 18 years I was made into what I am. (My parents are responsible. I didn't even ask to be born.) I am what I am and that's it. I was made into what I am by an external force.

Another person might answer the same question with, "I grew up in Slippery Rock." Or, "I spent my childhood in Slippery Rock." That person is implying that growing up is something he/she did, not something done unto him/her. It makes a difference which assumption you make when you decide who's responsible for what you have become.

Being an "acorn" and believing that I have choice, I find it logical to accept the fact that I'm responsible for me, my mental activity and my feelings. Because I have choice I can have intentions. I choose what I intend. I am responsible for the intentions behind my behavior. I'll be accountable for that. But I won't be answerable for your reactions or feelings because they result from **your** mental activity and the interpretation you chose which created the meaning and feeling for you.

If I say something which was not intended to hurt you, but you misinterpret my intention and create a hurtful meaning, then that is your responsibility. I won't design my behavior around my guess as to just what misinterpretation you might come up with. And I won't feel guilty. If I notice that you are feeling hurt, I will probably explain my intention. That would only be kindness. (I don't advocate cruelty to you, but I won't allow you to lay a guilt-trip on me.)

If you are hurt by something someone says, I suggest you say, "Ouch, that hurt." Then take time to figure out what you were doing in your own head that created a hurtful meaning. Or, you can ask the other person, "I feel hurt, was that your intention?" Then you can get down to the nitty gritty and really communicate. If you do, it will feel good.

I'll exercise my "response-ability" by trying to be responsive to others. I'll be responsible for the things I choose. That includes my intentions, my attitudes, what I allow in my mind and the feelings which result from that mental activity.

By defining my responsibilities and making a commitment to meet them, I feel as if I am in charge of my life. It feels good.

58

The Purpose of Life

When I was working with the graduate student who wanted to be a pro baseball player (See "Play Ball," Sec.I), something clicked inside me. It felt as if the insight, that we may all have the same purpose in life, was a significant idea which would be fun to play with. I started by playing with word definitions. In fact, I started with the word "word."

Word: A sound or symbol that communicates meaning. OK, what's meaning?

Meaning: Inner significance of something. Something that is felt.

Felt: To be emotionally affected by. To be aware of.

So that's one way of looking at words. They are vehicles for carrying meanings, which we become aware of through the emotional effects on us. I can believe that! Just think of the emotional effect of the F--- word! Other symbols are "loaded," too. The two fingers of the peace sign have one effect. But, if you retract the index finger, you get a totally different effect!

I'm reminded of when I moved off the farm and into Lincoln, Nebraska, to start the first grade. I had learned a new symbol at school that day. With all ten kids and my mother at the dinner table I showed off my new symbol, the meaning of which I knew not. I thumbed my nose at my brother. Quick as a flash I was on the back porch with Ivory soap in my mouth. I didn't learn the meaning of the symbol, but I certainly knew it had **power**. Obviously Mom knew the meaning and was emotionally affected by it!

Back to words.

Goal: Purpose toward which an endeavor is directed.

Purpose: A result or effort that is intended or desired.

Endeavor: A concerted effort toward a given end.

Assuming that I have choices in my life, and I choose to assume that I **do** have choices, I can choose to make a concerted effort intended to take me toward a desired end result which has significance and meaning for me. And that significance and meaning will be carried by words, which have an emotional component. So, when I trace through my goal and purpose in life, I end up with a **feeling**. Maybe, just maybe, we **do** all have the same purpose in life, to **feel good**.

Oh, yes, we want to make a difference in the world. We want to leave the world a better place. We want to be a good example for others. We want to help others. We want to feed the hungry. We want to leave a monument. We want to save souls. We want to relieve pain. We want to care for the sick and elderly. Or whatever. All wonderful goals. But secretly, in our innermost insides, don't we believe that if we can just do some of those things, then we will **feel good**? Maybe it **is** true, maybe our real purpose is to feel good.

How selfish! How self-centered! Shame, shame, guilt, guilt. What an awful idea!

Did you have a "shame" reaction to that idea? Many of us have learned that we are "bad" if we think of ourselves and our feelings first. Then, if we try to do something which might make us feel good, we get a "guilt" reaction and feel bad instead. If our real purpose is to feel good and we are blocked and frustrated by the guilt, it's no wonder so many people live guilt-filled rather than fulfilled lives.

So just hold it a minute before you put yourself down for wanting to feel good. What is so awful about that? We know that it is virtuous to make **others** happy. How could it be anything but virtuous to make **ourselves** happy?

I see life as a gift. The purpose of a gift is to create joy. So, the purpose of the gift of life is to create joy. If you see life as a pain in the neck, I'm certain that it is, for you. As the famous philosopher, Flip Wilson, used to say, "What you see is what you get."

Just making ourselves feel good spreads good vibrations around. Doing those virtuous projects, feeding the hungry, relieving pain, visiting the lonely, etc., can have a triple pay-off. Those projects **do** make the world a better place, and, knowing that, we feel good about having done them. Second, while performing one of those projects we create good feelings in the recipient (if they have learned to be gracious receivers). They feel good. And we can "catch" some of their good feeling through empathy or contagion. And, third, when others know of our good works, they can send us good vibes. I'm certain that the quality of the vibrations reflected back to Mother Theresa are of a much higher quality than the vibrations reflected back to Hitler and his men operating the death camps.

Whether feeling good is the direct goal in life, or the by-product of learning, growth, or good works, it adds the same positive quality to our lives.

The World Is My Classroom

I've found that a lot of things happen in a certain way because of my attitude, assumptions, posture or expectations. My inner attitude is represented by the way I stand, sit, fold my arms, my facial expression, my tone of voice and what I do with my eyes. The people I meet pick up these clues consciously or unconsciously and reflect them back. It seems to be the nature of people and even animals, that they can't help reflecting back. (Even a dog seems to know if I am afraid, or if I like or dislike dogs.) They seem to have little more choice than a mirror.

A high school sophomore I counseled demonstrated how this "reflecting back" can happen. She had just moved to town. She was afraid of being rejected by her new classmates. She said, "I knew how much that would hurt, so **I rejected them first**."

I'm reminded of the man who moved into a new neighborhood. He asked his neighbor what kind of people lived in that area. The neighbor asked about the type of people where he used to live. After hearing the description, the new neighbor confirmed that "you'll find people around here to be very much like those in the neighborhood you just left." I carry my mirror along with me and think I'm meeting new people. But a lot of what I'm meeting is just my old attitude, my expectations, my posture or stance.

If I think that life is a struggle, people can't be trusted, things always go wrong and people are out to get me, then that's the way it tends to work out. I'm always right, so it's difficult to change my mind. The way I approach the world sets the tone for how the world responds to me. And how the world responds to me triggers my feelings. So, my attitude, stance, posture or expectations are seeds that I plant. The seeds I sow determine the crop I harvest. I'd like to harvest a crop of good feelings, so I can take charge and choose my stance.

A most helpful stance, posture or attitude is to expect that THE WORLD IS MY CLASSROOM. It exists for my benefit. It wants me to succeed. It provides learning (which feels good). It fills my needs. It provides a place for me to express myself.

Any painful situation I unconsciously get myself into is really a mini-lesson. (Some of them are maxi-lessons!) It has been my observation that people often get themselves into painful situations. Then someone in the helping professions helps them get out of that situation. And within a few days or weeks they find themselves right back in a similar condition. I've asked social workers about this phenomenon. They say, "Oh, yes, it happens all the time." It's uncanny, as if we unconsciously insist on that type of an experience, until we learn how to handle that kind of a situation.

An adolescent girl can't stand her authoritarian father, so she runs away and gets married--to an authoritarian guy, nearly as old as her father. Or a woman marries one, two or three alcoholics (maybe a workaholic for variety). Then, when she learns how to relate to that type of person and not be an enabler, she can marry a different type. It's often the same with battered women. If you're having trouble with a person, ask yourself what you need to learn to make it tolerable. If you are an impatient person, the world will keep you waiting till you learn patience.

When "the world is your classroom" there are no social promotions. You get held back till you learn what you need to learn. Ask yourself, "What might I be learning?" When you get your answer, take charge and aim directly at that learning.

On Playing With Words

For a long time I've thought about the word "responsibility" as having the meaning, RESPONSE-ABILITY, the ability to respond to another person. That isn't too far from the meaning of "accountable" or "answerable." As I see it, one of my responsibilities is to respond to other people, to recognize them, to share with them, or allow them to share with me. That overcomes loneliness, affirms both of us and helps us learn and grow.

Another word I like to play with is "assume." When we communicate, you encode your message with your experiences. When I receive your message, I decode with my experiences. We assume that we understand what the other is saying, but we have different code books! We often misunderstand but don't take time to check it out. This makes an ASS out of U and Me. So please don't ASS-U-ME!

I don't enjoy the word INVALID. It has two meanings. One meaning implies that something is not legal, or is falsely based, or involves faulty reasoning. We have no right to hang that kind of a meaning on a person with a disability.

While we are creating new words, we certainly need new possessive pronouns to replace "my," "mine," and "our." According to usage we "own" our children, spouses and husbands in the same way that we own clothes, cars or other possessions. Now that's an assumption which can lead to trouble!

The term "therapist" can be divided in an interesting manner. A therapist who is not well put together can be THE-RAPIST.

To "atone" means to make amends for injury or wrong that was done. This reduces separation and gives us AT-ONE-MENT.

We are consciously aware of the surface meaning of words. Often there is a deeper, more powerful meaning which lies beneath the surface.

As you can see, I enjoy mind games and playing with words. It's probably because I had such a lousy beginning with baseball.

Modesty Is Dishonesty

In my youth if you wanted to be liked and accepted you had to be modest. That meant not being a braggard' and not being conceited. It also meant that you were to devalue or diminish your abilities, your performance or your worth. It meant to sell yourself short or put yourself down. As I listen to people, I'm convinced that many of them got the same message. Try to compliment some people and you get an argument or excuses.

"Your dress looks nice."

"Oh, this old rag. Got it on sale at Penneys years ago."

"That was a nice thing you did."

"It was nothing. The least I could do."

"You're really good at that."

"No. I was just lucky."

Along with being taught to be modest we were also taught to be honest and realistic. But it is difficult to be both modest and honest. Modesty is dishonesty. Modesty is pretending to be less than you are. At the least it is deceptive or a misrepresentation. If I ask you what you are modest about you may tell me that there is nothing you excel in. So we know that modesty has to do with excellence. It would seem ridiculous to be modest about one's mediocrities or inferiorities!

I think that those of us who feel inferior or inadequate don't want to hear the blatant self-approval of Mohammed Ali, the former Cassius Clay. It makes us uncomfortable. But he was honest. He was realistic. He **was** the greatest. That boxer went down in the record books for boxing. I put him down in my book for teaching millions of people that **it's OK to think highly of themselves**. Thanks, Mohammed.

On Motivation By Demons: Frightening Yourself Into Action

It is my own unofficial estimate that about 40% of the population motivate themselves by a negative "scare" tactic in order to get the juices flowing to start or complete a project. It seems to work but they pay a price in comfort and stress.

They tell themselves a scary story. "My husband will just kill me if I don't get his pants sewed up tonight." "Mom will be really angry if I stay out too late." "Dad will ground me if I don't get my assignment done."

They create an emergency which puts their body into the "fight or flight" condition, starting the adrenalin flowing. From the head down your body doesn't know if the emergency is real, like a truck bearing down on you as you cross the street, or a mad bull charging at you across the pasture. If it is a real emergency, the energy is there to jump or run to safety, like you've never run before! The energy is a life-saver and it is used up in saving your life. There are a lot of "super-strength" stories about people lifting up heavy objects to save a friend. My favorite is about a grandmother who was in a motorhome going through a safari country animal park. The door was open and a cougar jumped in and had the baby's head in his mouth. Grandmother, obviously full of adrenalin, grabbed a butcher knife off the counter and attacked the cougar driving him off. The child was saved, Grandma used up her adrenalin and the baby got about 17 inches of stitches. Fear can be a life saver. But if you use it to motivate yourself, you are living in a state of emergency a lot. And that is stressful.

When you are in a calm state, you can think of it as being at emotional ground zero, or emotional sea level. When you tell yourself a scary story, you dig a hole, go to the pits, get below emotional sea level.

You are now in negative territory. Your scary story is the

SEA ——————————————————— EMOTIONAL
LEVEL   FEELING   GROUND "O"
                                ARRIVAL
SCARY   ↓   "DRIVEN"   PROVIDES ONLY
STORY   RELIEF.
TOLD   ↓   ROUTE
TO SELF
PUTS YOU ↓   ESCAPE   GOAL IS ESCAPE
IN THE   FROM FAILURE, PAIN,
  PITS.   CRITICISM.
          ↓
DEMON   MOTIVATION — FEAR.

          A STATE OF EMERGENCY
          HAS BEEN CREATED.

             RESULT — STRESS.
THE "PITS"   UNHEALTHY

demon on your tail chasing you. You feel driven, motivated by fear, trying to escape from failure or punishment, in a state of emergency, stressed. When you do escape, if you do, you get back to zero, emotional sea level. There is a sense of relief, but not much satisfaction of achievement. You have been chased by your own demon to get back to where you started from before you frightened yourself.

You could skip the scary story and not use the demon or fear to motivate yourself. Pro athletes do not frighten themselves into a good performance. They "image" as clearly as possible what they want to achieve. Desire, not fear is the motivating factor. They are driving toward their goal, not being driven to escape from failure. And when they achieve their goal there is a sense of satisfaction, not just the relief of escaping from the demon.

During the recent Olympics, it was fun to watch Mary Lou Retton perform her gymnastic routine. She went from sea level to a great "high." She didn't put herself in the pits of fear. She enjoyed herself. She accomplished a lot, more than she could have with a demon chasing her. She felt good. To me it seems like the way to go.

* * * * *

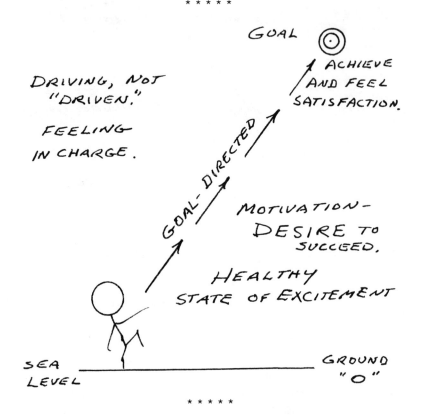

* * * * *

On Listening

Being listened to is a great feeling. Being understood is even greater. If I could be granted just one wish for the human race, it would be that we all be blessed with the ability (and inclination) to listen.

My fourth grade teacher in Riley grade school, Louise Anderton (What a jewel!), shared a thought with the class that has stuck with me. It was one of those "Aha!" experiences. (I find it interesting that I remember what she shared of herself, but not the subject matter.) She said that it is almost impossible to dislike a person if you listen to him/her long enough.

Now I understand that if I can listen and really hear, then I will become aware of the other person's memories, hopes, beliefs, thoughts and expectations. Then that person's life and how it is being lived will make sense to me. I'll quit judging, condemning and rejecting that person. What a solution for the problems of loneliness, violence, conflict, arbitration and mediation! But really listening is risky.

If I really listen I might change my ideas. That would mean that I was wrong before. (Mercy! It would also mean that I'm smarter now.) I would appear unreliable, weak, a push-over, wishy-washy, not having confidence in my knowledge, not having the courage of my convictions. (I might even have to find the courage to **change** my convictions.) Listening appears to be a passive rather than an active function. Active is good, like young. Passive is bad, like old. Don't kid yourself. If done properly, listening is about as mentally active as you can be.

One problem with talking/listening is that we can listen much faster than most people can talk. So the listener gets ahead of the talker or assumes from the first few words what is going to be said and then goes off on a mental side trip. Others spend that time rehearsing what they are going to say just as soon as it's their turn--and they can hardly wait. Sometimes they don't wait, they interrupt, which says, in effect, that the other person is not worth hearing.

A good listener will use the extra time to go back and review the first point, then the second, then the third. By the time the talker has finished, the listener may have a better outline than the speaker. To really be sure that he has heard, the listener will put the message in his own words to see if he really understands. What a joy, what a compliment, what a good feeling, when someone has listened to you so well that they can put your message or your feelings in their own words! Being understood feels so good and is so rare that clients sometimes associate that good feeling with their therapist and think they have fallen in love. They love being understood! That's what feels so good.

There is a powerful message in listening. It is, "You are **worth** listening to." That's a message worth sending.

Typically, we have classes in speech. Who ever had a class in listening? It's similar to the giving/receiving problem. It's more blessed to give than to receive. It's better to speak than to listen. So we have a lot of speakers and darn few listeners. Ever been to a cocktail party? The speakers are blasting away with words while the receivers are rehearsing what they are going to shout back. It's likely to get louder as the evening wears on. There appears to be a tremendous need to express, to get through to another person, to bridge our aloneness. Just talking does part of it. But the process is incomplete until you are heard, until real sharing takes place, or someone, somehow affirms that you exist.

I have a hunch that a lot of violence comes from that need to get through to another human being. (Pets are often a good substitute. They listen without interrupting.)

Years ago I read a news report about a young man in Phoenix. He went to a beauty parlor, made all 10 people in the place lie face down on the floor, then shot each of them in the back of the head. While waiting to be picked up by the police, he was heard to remark, "Now maybe someone will notice me."

I worked with a rape "victim" once. The first thing we did was to change her program from "victim" to a **person** who had experienced rape. (You are **not** what you do and you are **not** what is done to you.) Anyway, she wakened one very dark night with the point of a knife pressed against her throat. The man was lonely. He talked for 45 minutes. He still raped her. Thought she'd enjoy it. There was the need to talk, the need to penetrate, to "get through" to another human.

How much violence is frustrated communication? I don't know. A lot, I think. This idea first came to me after reading a report written by a man who was convicted of a stabbing. He described the physical release, the good feeling, he got when the knife penetrated, "got through." He was noticed. That need to communicate is strong. I can recall hearing myself say on several occasions, "I don't have to have my way, but I do have to have my say."

All frustrated communication need not end up in violence such as stabbing. Some people have "sharp" tongues with which they make "cutting remarks." Graffiti and vandalism may be a way to "talk back" to the school, the church or the government. It might be cheaper to listen and let people have their say.

Yes, I do believe that the gift of listening skills, and the desire to hear, would be just about the best gift the human race could receive.

On Love

I think "love" was an embarrassment to psychologists for several decades. Years ago I tried to find it in the index of several psychology books. All I found was a paragraph on glandular secretions! Those were the days when things didn't exist unless they could be measured. Today it seems absolutely appalling to think of psychology, the study of human behavior, without including love. Defining exactly what love is presents another challenge.

Harry Stack Sullivan said that when the satisfaction, security and development of another person becomes as significant to you as your own satisfaction, security and development, then love exists. Nelson M. Foote said that love is that relationship between one person and another which is most conducive to the optimum development of both. Sullivan seems to be describing a "caring" relationship while Foote requires that the relationship enhance the growth and development of both. Maybe when two or more are gathered together in a caring relationship love is present. (That sounds like Love is God or God is Love.)

Since I feel inadequate to try and define God today, I'll stick with a description of some of the dimensions or components of love that seem true for me:

1. Feelings of respect for and pride in the independence, individuality, growth and development of another. Brotherly love.

2. A spontaneous outgoing or overflowing warmth and affection. The full bucket, the cup that runneth over, the need to **give** love.

3. Erotic, physical, sensual, sexual feelings.

4. Desire, longing, hunger, the empty bucket, the need to **receive** love.

5. A sense of closeness, oneness, intimacy, trust, confidence in the absence of erotic feelings. Motherly love.

6. Contact comfort, the need to touch and be touched. Tactile sensory input. Pets, teddy bears, Linus' blanket.

7. Feelings of hostility. Resentment toward the person from whom one wanted, needed and thought they deserved love. ("I hate my father. All I ever wanted was for him to love me.")

8. A choice, a decision, a commitment to always care for another regardless of what he/she might do. Unconditional love.

9. An energy which enhances growth as well as physical and mental health. It feels good, as in a hug.

In addition to all of those dimensions, I believe that love is incompatible with fear, and that it is contagious. But we don't know how it works. Some believe it doesn't work. Many see love as impractical, idealistic, an opiate. Some see loving as being a "wimp," a weakling, a door mat which invites being walked on. The people with the **need** for love (#4), with the deficiency of love, may allow themselves to be abused, battered and walked on in order to receive some little bit of attention, a scrap or a crumb. But that isn't love, it's the absence of, and the need for, love.

Pitirim Sorokin was hunted down by the Russian Communist government in 1918 and condemned to death. For four years he witnessed the shooting of his friends and observed endless horrors of bestiality, death, and destruction. He survived and so did his confidence in the power of love. At Harvard University 35 years later he still maintained that, "Love is the most powerful antidote against criminal, morbid, and suicidal tendencies; against hate, fear, and psychoneuroses." Love can work.

But if love **does** work, we would be wise to be using it. We don't need to know **how** it works. Most of us don't understand how aspirin works but we use a lot of it! Come to think of it, if we tried love we might not need so much aspirin!

On Skin Hunger

A few years ago I read SEX: IF I DIDN'T LAUGH I'D CRY by Jess Lair, PhD. A lot of things in the book registered, but the idea of "skin hunger" clicked the most. Jess said he thought that a lot of prostitution was really due to a need for more touch. You'll remember from the essay "On Love" (this section) that love is necessary for survival and that touch is one dimension or component of love.

In the 1920's a famous psychologist recommended that we not cuddle the little ones. A pat on the head at bedtime was as far as a parent was to go. There were infants who died mysteriously. In one hospital, infants less than one year old were booked-in as "terminal." Just as mysteriously, infants started to survive. The mystery was solved when it was discovered that the night cleaning lady carried the babies around on her hip while doing her work. She had a need to give love. The babies needed to receive it. The two problems fit together nicely as one solution.

When I had clients who seemed to need one affair after another, I'd ask if they really wanted sex. Nearly 100% said no, they just wanted to be close and to be held. It isn't just infants who need touching. (What an interesting study could be done with employees of massage parlors, legitimate and otherwise, and prostitutes.) The need for touch never ends. I've done a few presentations at nursing homes. When I shook hands with the people, they didn't want to let go. They just held my hand, as if they were starving to touch another person.

I remember reading about and seeing a videotape of the Tasaday group in the Philippine Islands. When discovered in 1971 they were still living in the stone age. There were about 30 of them and they had achieved a balance with their environment.

Officials from Manila helicoptered in to study them. You

74

never saw such a loving, touching bunch. One of the visitors was bald. The Tasadays liked to feel his head. The older boys would slide down a mud bank, each with a smaller child sitting on his bare shoulders. They enjoyed each other. They were civilized, even without indoor plumbing. But the most "civilized" part of the report was that the Tasaday didn't know what conflict was. Never a fight or a murder. They had no words that pertained to conflict.

Note: I had the opportunity to hear John Nance recently. As a journalist he has been studying the Tasaday group for 15 years and has written three books about them. There are claims that the whole affair is a hoax. He finds no conclusive evidence of that. In fact, the very presence of their language is powerful evidence that they are not a hoax. However, various interests would like access to their territory. There would be no need to continue to protect them if the whole deal was a hoax.

Are humans basically loving creatures, or naturally hostile and aggressive? How you decide to believe on that question will make a lot of difference on who gets your vote. How congress believes will affect the budget deficit. Incidently, have you hugged your kids today? Or your congressman?

Love Thy Neighbor As Thyself

I think this exhortation has been badly distorted. For some people I think it meant that you **should** love your neighbor, it was your duty. And that **should**, like all shoulds, implied that you were not OK unless you **did** love your neighbor. You had to love your neighbor first. But even then it was not OK to love yourself.

Remember Cassius Clay when he just came on the scene in the world of boxing. He would get on TV and recite poems and say how great he was. People were indignant. "Who does he think he is?" His self-love made a lot of Christians very uncomfortable. He was "conceited." That was a no-no. You were supposed to be modest, which meant to put yourself down, to verbally diminish yourself. Seeing his blatant self-approval made a lot of us uncomfortable with our own feelings of inadequacy. It seemed obvious that it was OK to love others but **not** yourself.

The problem with this is that the standard, the guideline, the manner in which you are to love your neighbor is the way in which you love yourself--which is a no-no.

I wish the translation had been, "Love yourself so that you can love your neighbor." Then there would be no bind. It would be such a natural thing to do. We know from experimental psychology that if our response to one stimulus is to love, then our response to a similar stimulus is likely to be to love. Since you are similar to me, if my response to me is love, then my response to you is likely to be love. There's no bind there. That could work. At least it's worth a try. If you don't already love yourself, you can take charge and start right now. You can choose to care about yourself, no matter what happens to you. The power is yours.

On Jealousy

Jealousy is basically fear. It's the fear of losing the one who fills your bucket, the one who makes you feel good. It exists when there is a deficiency of love, when the bucket of love and approval is near empty.

If you are into putting yourself down and condemning yourself for mistakes or shortcomings, you are emptying your own bucket. You need approval to survive, so you have to get it from others since you seem to give yourself only **disapproval**. Jealousy can be seen as a measure of love. But it is more accurately seen as a dependency and the fear of losing the source of love or approval. Jealousy can be seen as an addiction, the jealous one being the addict, the other person being the fix. The fix then becomes an object, a possession (**my** girl). Jealousy is possessive. The source of approval must be protected from potential competition. Jealousy "smothers" the person with constant watching and checking until he/she says, "Give me some space, let me up for air." The relationship, being held tight like the frog, dies.

If you are the fix for a jealous person, face the reality that you are being used, that you may be serving as an enabler for the addict. If you take charge and break off the relationship don't be surprised if your professed true love finds a new source within a day or two.

If you are the jealous one, stop putting yourself down. Realize that you are an OK person. Help fill your own bucket and refuse to depend totally on others. You may not be able to fix your feelings of inadequacy without help, but you can get started on the project. Choose to care about yourself. Take that power, it is yours. And do things you'll like yourself for having done.

On Anger and Hurt

Anger can generate a lot of energy. It can be exhilarating. It feels like strength, but it doesn't make the mind bright. It shuts off the ability to think clearly, or to think at all. Did you ever hear the expression "blind rage"? That's not exactly a problem-solving state of mind.

A lot of anger comes from frustration of a desire or goal. Some blankety blank won't let you complete what you want to do. But I think that most anger is a cover-up, a substitute for hurt.

You can express anger and ventilate it by talking, yelling, pounding, or writing. One lady didn't want to pound on her mother but she said she would enjoy choking her. So I rolled up a towel just neck size and let her burn off the energy that way and get rid of the feeling and its control over her.

If anger is a cover-up for hurt, and the hurt isn't expressed, the anger is likely to surface over and over. Hurt can be discharged by weeping, crying, sobbing, writing or talking. A good way to get in touch with the hurt is to look into the eyes of another person and just say, "It hurts!" Or, you can describe the knot in the stomach until the knot loosens and goes away.

It is very easy to get confused when discharging or ventilating anger. Saying, "It hurts!" is describing the hurt. But saying, "He had no right to do that to me, it isn't fair!" **creates** more anger. There are two steps to handling anger. First, discharge what you've accumulated. Then you can think more clearly. Second, find out what mental activity created the anger in the first place and stop that activity ("The Big Lie" Sec. II). Anger causes lots of problems in relationships. Take charge and fix it.

On Depression

This is a tough one. It has such a range of possibilities from feeling low to a very active dedication to end it all. Sometimes physical restraint is necessary. It may be a chemical imbalance. (That's the first thing to check out with your doctor.) I'll only skim the surface and mention some possibilities, a few of which may be new to you.

Anger that is created and not ventilated or given expression but turned inward is a common source of depression. People with this habit may believe that showing anger is immature, undignified, sinful, or all of the above. They may have been punished severely as children for losing their tempers. They have to be "nice." However, once they can admit the presence of anger (and the hurt which is often there, too), then they can work through the feelings either alone or with a helper. Writing, talking, yelling, pounding, weeping, crying and/or swearing can assist in discharging the stored up emotional energy of the past.

Negative self-talk or "stinking thinking" can produce depression. Playing "ain't it awful" and focusing on all of the rotten stuff in the world (listening to too many TV news broadcasts); or focusing on all that is wrong with self (I'm no good, you're no good, the world is a lousy place, it's a dog-eat-dog existence, a rat-race, people can't be trusted, why was I ever born!) can be depressing. Playing "poor me" and crawling into your own little "pity bag" are natural depressants.

I've found sometimes that people can put themselves into the pits by having a feeling about having a feeling. The scenario goes something like this:

I'm feeling sad. I have no right to be sad. Things are going OK. What's wrong with me? I shouldn't be feeling this way. It isn't fair! This really makes me angry. But I have no right to be angry. I wish I knew what's wrong with me. Its frustrating not knowing what is wrong with me. I suppose I'll never know. It seems so hopeless. I can't stand this much longer. I'm so upset I can barely function. When will it ever end? I can't think. I can't sleep. I'd better take some valium or sleeping pills or something so that I can at least get to work tomorrow.

Why not say to self, "OK, self, I'm sad right now. That's interesting. Is my inner guide, my unconscious mind, trying to tell me something? Let me 'focus' (See Gendlin on FOCUSING) for a while and see if I can learn what's eating on me." You could learn some surprising things.

A fellow psychologist told me about a trucker he worked with who was depressed most of the time. Just by accident, the psychologist learned that the man spent hours and hours on the road listening to the saddest cowboy songs he could find. They all reminded him of the wife who left him. He was in perpetual mourning. When he got his grief out properly, the old "unfinished business" got finished and his depression lifted.

Unresolved grief is a common source of depression. It is often overlooked as the years go by and it never occurs to anyone that the loss is still affecting that person. Until we really listen to a person we don't know what constitutes a "loss" for them. It could be a teddy bear, or a dog, or a pony. I worked with a woman once who still missed her stuffed tiger. It was old and ragged and dirty when her folks threw it away without her permission. But that old tiger had given comfort to this person (touch is a part of love) and had listened patiently as she poured out her heart and soul to it. On another occasion it was a real live pony that had been the listener who accepted the client unconditionally and thus earned her love. But the most touching, for me, was the little girl who was sexually and physically abused by her father and emotionally and psychologically abused by her mother. She found a tree which she could climb. It had a nearly horizontal limb which she could lie on and hug. She talked to the tree, shared with it, invested in it emotionally. **Nobody** ever understood why she cried when they cut it down. In reality, that tree was her very own loving, caring, accepting mother; and one heck of a lot more nurturing than her biological mother was able to be.

Another source of depression due to unresolved grief comes from miscarriages. It is easy to overlook the loss of the fetus and the relationship which had already developed with the mother. Sometimes there is also a relationship with the father. Abortion often constitutes a loss which calls for grieving. It is complicated further by the guilt which may be involved and the additional guilt heaped on by groups which harass abortion centers. Even having the baby and giving it up for adoption is a loss which must be dealt with. Unmarried women who get pregnant or married women who get pregnant through an affair have a special problem of secrecy when they try to grieve their loss after a miscarriage or abortion.

The 75 year old man in "I Killed My Father" was certainly suffering from the depression of unresolved grief as well as a lot of guilt. The lady in "I Had a Baby Out of Wedlock" also had some depression as she worried about her 18 year old son coming to her door.

Even exercise, or the lack of it can contribute to depression. I remember getting a call from a lady who was so depressed that I could just barely hear her. She was so "down" that I could imagine that she was barely breathing. I asked her to stand up. Then raise her right foot in the air, then the left. By the time she was walking in place, I could hear her clearly. Then I had her jog. That helped a lot to lift the depression. Exercise helps. Get up and do something. Move that body. Get the blood to circulating to the head. Breathe deeply.

Another but a very different source of depression involves what we take into our bodies. Poor nutrition can have a depressing effect on a person. Ever hear of the "Sugar Blues"? David Sheinkin, MD, and others have a book entitled FOOD, MIND & MOOD.

What we take into our bodies includes the air and what comes with it. The the air we breathe can dampen our mood or sense of well-being if it has a high positive ion concentration. This can occur near mountains in various parts of the world, or it can happen in the "processed" air which we breathe in an air conditioned building. In these cases the proportion of positive ions to negative ions gets too high. Negative ions help people feel better. You can get more negative ions in the shower, near a waterfall, or in front of an open fireplace. Commercial negative ion generators are available. One of the books is THE ION EFFECT by Fred Soyka.

Another item which we take into our bodies is sunlight. Research is being conducted now at the Oregon Health Sciences University in Portland. They call it SAD, Seasonal Affect Disorder. There is a lot of sunshine in Portland, but it comes mostly during one six-month period. They had a lot of volunteers for this project. During the rainy season, the participants in the study exposed themselves daily to several minutes of full spectrum fluorescent light. A few experienced a near miraculous recovery from seasonal depression. Several years ago John N. Ott, the time-lapse photography expert, broke his glasses and learned a lot about sunlight and artificial light, and their effects. Ott discovered the need for full spectrum light. (Later research links production of the hormone melatonin to sunlight.) Ott's book is HEALTH AND LIGHT.

You may have read a few years ago about the Russians aiming an energy beam at our embassy in Moscow and producing illness in the people who worked there. I don't know much about this and I have no books on it yet, but I'm alerted to look for anything on ELF or Extremely Low Frequency radiation or transmission. It is reported to have an effect on the protein molecules of the body as well as an effect on the emotions. One of the interesting characteristics of ELF is that it dissipates very little with distance. That reminds me of the Russian experiment I wrote about where there was communication between the mother rabbit in the laboratory and her babies in the submarine which was out of radio range (see "On Abortion" in this section). Maybe thought transmission and ELF both have the characteristic of not dissipating with distance. If so, another powerful force is available for us to use. Like most all of our discoveries, I expect that it could be used to hurt or help, to kill or cure. It's stuff for the back burner, at least for now.

These mysterious vibes and radiations remind me that emotions are contagious and that we can catch them from those around us. Not everyone is that sensitive to the feelings of others, but some are. Most of us can feel the tensions when it is "thick enough to cut it with a knife." Others may be like the dentist in "There's Nothing I Can Do" who seemed to be picking up the fear and tension of his patients. I think that depression is sometimes transmitted from one to another in the same way. We all know people who "make us sick" or drain our energy. It might be a good idea to use Boswell's mentally produced bubble of light, or get away from them quickly!

Another source of depression has to do with "people" or energy systems who give out bad vibes even after they have left their bodies permanently. I'm convinced that some very interesting (but unseen) things go on about us. I believe much of what we call mental illness has something to do with this unseen stuff; the "unclean spirits" of the Bible, multiple personalities (THREE FACES OF EVE, SYBIL, THE MINDS OF BILLY MILLIGAN), reincarnation, obsession, possession, exorcism, and that whole bag of ancient, interesting but as yet unexplained material.

I've tried to piece it together this way. If each personality is an energy system, and energy cannot be destroyed, then there are a lot of energy systems floating around. Some are happy, some are depressed. Some are angels and some are SOB's. Some are dead and don't realize it. They get into the energy system of a live person and try to run that physical body. Maybe several get in and take turns! I've read about that in THIRTY YEARS AMONG THE DEAD by Carl A Wickland, MD, who was in charge of a mental institution in the Chicago area starting about 1906. It is a fascinating report of a lifetime of working with the spirits of deceased people who were attached to the energy systems of his mental patients. He dislodged the spirits with a static electricity generator, the design of which came to him in a dream. His wife was a medium and was able to allow the spirits to speak through her.

Well, I guess by now you know why I said that this was a tough one. We have gone from repressed anger to negative self-talk to sad songs to unresolved grief to exercise to nutrition to ions to a lack of sunlight to ELF radiation to the attachment of depressed or unclean spirits. That's a real mixed bag! What to do?

First, be certain that you don't have a chemical imbalance.

See your doctor.

If you have repressed anger, give yourself permission to be angry, to talk angrily, to write angrily, to scream, yell or pound. Write out old resentments, but don't mail them. (You need to spit them out, but not directly on the resentee!) When you get rid of the anger, then you can forgive. Next, figure out how you made yourself angry in the first place, so you can stop doing that. You can handle grief in much the same way.

Cut out the negative self-talk. Pick some "up" songs to replace the perpetual sadness variety. Set up an exercise routine and follow it. Eat right. Get out of depressing surroundings. (Kids, go clean up your room! Mothers, close the door to their rooms.) Get a negative ion generator (but get one with a positive plate to attract all of the pollution or you will get soot deposits at the nails under the plaster in the walls). Go for a walk on a sunny day and take off your glasses. Surround yourself with a bubble of love and light, then hope for the best.

If all of this taking charge of your feelings hasn't helped, see a consultant in the mental health field.

On Forgiveness

If there is someone in your life whom you haven't forgiven you are working overtime. Carrying around a gunny sack of resentment is heavy--and corrosive! Every time you think of that person, up comes your blood pressure, tension, and stomach acid. That is giving a lot of power to someone you don't even like. You are handcuffed to all of those memories and negative

* * * * *

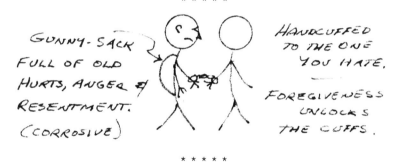

GUNNY-SACK
FULL OF OLD
HURTS, ANGER &
RESENTMENT.
(CORROSIVE)

HANDCUFFED
TO THE ONE
YOU HATE.

FOREGIVENESS
UNLOCKS
THE CUFFS.

* * * * *

feelings which you must preserve in order to enjoy your delicious condemnation. And **you** are the one who pays the price and carries the weight.

I worked with a nun once who believed that she had been betrayed by another nun who was her supervisor. She was still really ticked-off 18 years later. In my office she got down to the nitty-gritty. She talked out her anger and hurt, pounded the ever-ready cushion and used words that I was surprised that she knew. When she finished she understood why her Lord had instructed her, "Do not let the sun set on your anger." That's 6,574 sunsets. She came back the next week looking quite relaxed. She said it was difficult to believe the relief she received after forgiving her supervisor. It was "like living underwater for 18 years and then coming to the surface."

Another lady was a battered wife. After she discharged the pain and anger, she forgave her former husband. She took off the handcuffs. The divorce alone didn't separate her from him. She even came to realize that it was a good thing that he had hit her so hard the last time because it awakened that little spark of dignity in her which said "enough." Then she got up off the floor and started putting her life together. If he'd been just a little more gentle with his abuse she might still be the floor mat and the punching bag.

(Have you noticed that more of my clients are female? About two-thirds is the average. The men tend to ignore their feelings-- and die seven years younger.)

Another task for many is forgiving parents who have been negligent or abusive, or who haven't lived up to their children's expectations of what a parent **should** be. If you have any old hurts, anger or disappointments, you will lighten-up and feel better if you can express them and get rid of them. You need to get them out. Your parent(s) have no need to hear those old feelings, so don't attack them in person. If you do attack, you just create backlash in the form of hurt for them and guilt for you. Just vomit it out of your system. If you haven't forgiven someone, you aren't as well as you could be. MAKING PEACE WITH YOUR PARENTS by Harold Bloomfield, MD, is a recent paperback which could be very helpful. Why not try it? Take charge. You'll feel a lot better.

If you are a parent, you might ask for forgiveness. My Mom did that on her Christmas card in 1975:

> I had a dream last night which bro't back memories of times past when I was harsh and unreasonable in my treatment of you kids when you were growing up. I thought you had to be punished for things that displeased me when love and understanding were what was really needed.
>
> I don't know why it had never before occurred to me to tell you how sorry I am for all such times and I hope to be forgiven.
>
> It seems that Christmas might be a good time to tell you that I love you all dearly, including the wives and husbands who have been added to our Johnston clan. I am sorry for any misunderstandings we may have had and I am truly grateful for all the love and happiness you have given to me.
>
> You have taught me many things and I trust that I will continue to learn. It has been a joy to see the different ones developing & taking places of responsibility and usefulness in the world.
>
> Love,
> Mom

86

After that we laughed about the time she washed my mouth out with Ivory soap for innocently thumbing my nose at my brother during supper when I was in the first grade. But she never did admit to knowing exactly what that gesture meant!

On Handguns and Hot Tempers

For years I kept an article that I had clipped out of Time magazine. It was on the subject of handguns. I remember being very excited when a psychiatrist from New York described the problem accurately as our inablility to handle our anger. I expected him to say something about the way in which we cause our own anger, how to handle it, and maybe even how handling anger could be taught in school. I was disappointed. He went on about handguns!

The assumption seems to be that if we eliminated handguns, we could eliminate domestic violence. Not true! Domestic violence is not caused by handguns. The handgun is a convenient tool to express that violence. If the handgun is eliminated, killing the person who "caused" our anger will be a bit more inconvenient. We will have to hit, choke or stab with the kitchen knife. That will be more personal and might reduce the mayhem slightly. But the root of the violence will remain as it has always been: the generation of anger and the subsequent inability to control it or express it harmlessly.

Eliminating the handgun because anger goes out of control makes about as much sense as eliminating kleenex when the cold germs go out of control. (You'll just find another device to wipe your nose on, like when you were a kid and used your sleeve!)

I have a tiny arsenal in my closet. It has been there for 33 years when I went to Guam and left the family in a new neighborhood amongst rumors of prowlers. Last year I even got new bullets for my .22 revolver because an ex-boyfriend was threatening my daughter's life. (Twenty years ago I could have whipped him. Now I appreciate the little equalizer.)

It's nice to have a little power. If absolute power corrupts, I don't think we should give all the power to our protectors. It **could** corrupt them. It seems like good judgment to protect the boundaries of the home as well as the homeland. But I wouldn't fill the house with munitions. That would be creating a **hazard** in the home, not safety. (We may have created a hazard in the homeland by accumulating enough destructive power to wipe out the world several times.)

Besides the handgun, another lethal weapon is that 3,000 pound projectile, the automobile. Drivers have been killing people with it for many years. The average for the past 40 years has been between 40,000 and 50,000 per year. I don't know how many of the drivers who had accidents were suffering from uncontrolled anger. I suspect that many were angry. They were allowed possession of that lethal weapon after taking a written test on the rules, an eye test and a driving test. But no sanity test! Many police departments train their people to control their emotions while being subjected to badgering, abusive language and insults. The same training could be used for those who want to own handguns. Maybe we should test potential owners of handguns to determine if they understand the source of their emotions and have the ability to control them. I think it's worth a try. Problems just don't get solved until we get to the root. The root of this problem is handling the anger, not the handgun.

On Mob Reactions

Lying in bed this morning I was thinking about mob violence. (No, there was no mob in my bed.) I was led to this, I suppose, by my recent thoughts about the contagious nature of our emotions and how our emotional energy fields overlap and affect those close to us. I thought about the athletic events which get out of control, such as the European Cup soccer final in Brussels in May, 1985. The September 12, 1986 issue of THE CHRISTIAN SCIENCE MONITOR (yesterday) had an article on Sgt. Mary Farrell and her job of cooling heated emotions in a crowded sports arena. The same article mentioned that last month an angry fan threw a knife at a player in Yankee Stadium. (Elimination of handguns doesn't eliminate anger!)

I also thought about the mixing of the energy fields and how good it feels for two people who care about each other to hug each other. Then I recalled some of the classes and groups I'd been in where real trust and sharing had developed. Graduate students used to say that they were tired at 7:00 PM when the class started, but by 10:00 PM they were energized. Some of the classes had class reunions. Many friendships developed. I know of some that go back 15 years or more.

Now come thoughts about the dentist and all of the pain and fear vibes in his office that he was picking up. Then the mental hospitals where the most disturbed patients are grouped together and probably escalate their own disturbed conditions by combining them. Then the hospitals where all of the pain and fear is accumulated, and what a deterrent that must be when a person is trying to get well, or at least to get to feeling good.

I read about an experiment once where a subject was put in a room and given an electric shock. Two rooms down the hall at a distance of about 40 feet another subject sat with the instructions to press a button at the moment when he/she believed that the other person had been shocked. As it worked out, the one trying to guess the time of the shock was not successful. However, the "guesser's" brain was wired up, and the moment the other person felt pain, a blip showed up in the brainwave of the guesser. Even though the effect was not conscious, there was an unconscious effect of one person's pain on another person's brain. In "On Abortion" (this section) I wrote of the Russian experiment wherein the mother's body reacted when each of her babies was killed aboard the distant submarine. I'm convinced. The emotions of one person can affect another person. That effect is multiplied by large numbers whether the emotion is positive or negative.

Religious revivals often display the contagious effects of positive emotions. But the most impressive display of "mob" caring was the Olympics in Los Angeles. All of those young people celebrating life and enjoying each other (and themselves) was a sight I'll never forget. We ought to show it once a year just to remind us of what is possible between people and between nations.

On Drugs

We are about to spend a big bundle of money in a war on drugs. (We can't seem to get motivated to do anything without calling it a "war" and having an enemy.) Right now we are afraid of drugs. Crack is cheap and plentiful. We are afraid of it. Congress will spend money on what it fears, whether it is poverty, pollution, cancer, communism or crack. Drugs are not the enemy. Drugs are harmless until a person uses them. The pushers may seem like the enemy. But they are engaged in a lucrative, exciting, dangerous, illegal free enterprise system which comes into being whenever a demand exists. The root cause is the **demand**.

Why do people demand drugs? Some get hooked because they are curious, or they may have been tricked into their early experiments. But most people take drugs because it makes them **feel good**. The more pain people feel, the more they'll pay to feel good. The real question, then is just **why do so many people feel so bad?**

There are many reasons. Some have to do with self esteem. People don't like, respect, or value themselves. Sometimes they learn in school that they are "failures." I think that every child can be good at something and feel good about that. A few schools take time to look for each child's area of excellence. The Valley, Nebraska, schools (where my brother, John, is Superintendent) have a program which does that. I've seen little geniuses who could dangle their teachers on the edge of a nervous breakdown. That is genius, and it ought to be recognized and respected. Then that talent should be redirected.

The competitiveness of our society seems to create a few winners but a lot of "losers." You are somebody if you win. You are nobody if you lose. I find it very moving to watch an entire city celebrate the winning of a pennant or the superbowl. So many of the inhabitants of the city appear in front of the TV cameras after the final game, cheering loudly and holding up one finger for #1. They seem to be saying, "I was a nobody, but now we have won and I am a **somebody**!" I'm saddened that they never learned that they have always been important, unique and valuable. If someone will listen to them and love them, they might begin to get the idea that they are worth listening to, and worth loving. We don't need to create a "war" to do that.

Another source of pain which drugs might kill is the pain of being a "have not." It's related to self esteem. I can remember the pain of having an old 1930 model A Ford when the 1936's came out. I can still see that cream colored one I wanted my father to buy. Then I would feel like I was somebody. I wanted that car so much I could almost taste it. Now I enjoy old cars as well as new ones, but I don't **have to have** a new one to feel good. Just as we confuse our performance with our human worth, we confuse our possessions with our worth. The drug user turned pusher is very likely to buy one or more expensive cars with the profits of his/her enterprise. Then he/she will be "looked up to."

I just thought of the Tasaday group in the Philippines. They were a "have not" society. But they were joyous sliding down a mud bank. I remember some sage saying that richness can be an abundance of things or a scarcity of wants.

As long as people don't like themselves, there will be psychological pain. As long as there is psychological pain there will be a demand for pain-killers, the **fast, fast relief** we hear about on TV many times a day. Drugs are the symptom. The root of the problem is **not feeling good.**

How Can I Ever Trust You Again?

The awful thing has been done. It has been found out. The fight has taken place. I have forgiven you for being awful, for hurting me, for letting me down, for destroying my trust. Now, how can I ever trust you again? How can you **earn** my trust? How can you ever **deserve** my trust?

I've got you where I want you and I'll make you pay and pay. You'll suffer the way I had to. I have forgiven but I will never be able to forget what you have done to me.

You are not going to be OK, worthy of trust, until I say you are. The fight may be over, but the punishment has just begun. This relationship will be full of pain and frustration. The one trying to earn trust never knows how much is still due on the account. It's like blackmail. Frustrating. The one who supposedly wants to trust is still full of resentment and hasn't really forgiven the other. Sick.

This situation is like many others involving people who cannot allow themselves to ventilate their anger. The anger and the hurt associated with it stays inside and interferes with the process of forgiveness. The system is clogged up and the poison can't be released.

One person **insisting** that the resultant **effect** on him or her was the planned **intention** of the other person makes the pain more intense, forgiveness more difficult, vengeance sweeter and trusting out of the question. Under these conditions trust will probably never be earned.

Now if I change the "inner attitudes" of my mind, I should be able to change the "outer aspects" of my life. Let's try a different approach. I see what you did as thoughtless, meaning without thought or premeditated intention to hurt or humiliate me. I have suffered a disappointment and perhaps the permanent loss of a relationship. For that loss I will grieve. I'll ventilate my hurt and anger harmlessly in a way which will not inflict pain on others. I refuse to give you the power to "make a fool of me" or to diminish me in any way. Your action reflects on you, not me. I will not be the "victim" of your behavior. I will not use trust as contract, a deal or a bargaining chip to get you to refrain from certain behaviors, or to control you. Controlling you is **your** job. I will not torture myself by asking what I did wrong to cause this awful thing to happen. I will survive and learn and grow in my classroom. I will forgive because I want my mind to be free of resentment. I will not waste my creative mental energy on hatred. Forgiving is a **choice** which I have the power to make. How can I ever trust you again? If I want to be a trusting person, I can **choose** to trust you. I'm in charge of my life.

The key to making all of this possible consists of remembering and really **knowing** that the behavior of another person **in no way diminishes me**. Or, as Gerald Jampolsky, MD, says in LOVE IS LETTING GO OF FEAR, "Other people do not have to change for me to achieve peace of mind."

Anything Worth Doing Is Worth Doing Poorly

I'll bet you think I got it wrong. Right? You heard it this way, "Anything worth doing is worth doing well." Most of the perfectionists I've run into have this "is worth doing well" version firmly planted in their belief system. I've had a lot of experience with this one because therapists tend to see a lot of perfectionists.

They're never satisfied with themselves, their friends, relatives or the world in general. They know that everything **should** be perfect. They also know that nothing and nobody is perfect. So they have a sure-fire system for defeat and frustration.

The perfectionists who think their performance has to be perfect set themselves up for defeat also. They seem to reason that if they can't do something well, then they shouldn't even try. Of course, if they can't do any of the things worth doing, they end up doing nothing, or just those things **not worth doing** at all. This makes their lives boring, dull and without meaning.

Perfectionists would be happier if they realized that perfection is not a destination. To arrive at perfection would be stagnation. No more learning, no more growing. Perfecting is a process, not a destination.

You are already the perfect "you." Nobody can be you like you can. If others try to be you they will fail. If you try to be "not-you" you'll be a phony.

Take charge. Mess up. Get experience. But **learn** from doing poorly and do it less poorly the next time. Eventually you will be able to do it well. Remember, to you it is **worth** doing, so it will bring some meaning into your life. That ought to feel good.

My Ideal Is An Eye-deal

Have you ever been called an "idealist" and told that something was impractical or unrealistic? I have, so I've done some thinking about it.

To me, it seems as if the recommenders of the realistic and practical are saying, "Let's aim so low that we can't possibly miss." That doesn't seem like a practical way to make progress. I guess I'd rather fail at something significant than to succeed at something that didn't make any difference.

I've worked it out this way. I want an ideal, humane, soft-hearted goal. I don't want my ideal so high that my head is in the clouds and obscures my ability to see where I'm going. I do want my feet solidly on the ground so that I can make some progress toward my goal. Feet on the ground is the practical part. That's where I want them. But I want my vision, my eyes, below the clouds but high enough to see my goal. I don't want my "vision" to be so high that I can't reach it or so low that I can't miss it. And it certainly wouldn't be very practical to have my eyes down there on my toes! To be practical and make progress, you have to attempt what is thought to be impossible, like the 4-minute mile.

I like the soft heart to pick the goal and a hard head to make progress toward that goal. The hazard with a soft heart is that it's so easy to slide into having a soft head and making no progress. The hard heart and the hard head can make progress like a Hitler. And the hard heart with the soft head belong to the pessimistic cynic who goes no place but just sits there and bitches about how awful everything is.

I want my vision, my eye-deal, to be high enough to see where I'm headed while my feet are on solid ground.

On Mistakes

There's no such thing as a mistake. It's just a label, a pain-producing label which makes a person feel rotten, discouraged, frustrated, angry, or all of the above. If you use that label on yourself, you'll get some fall-out of negative feelings. Your labeling something a "mistake" is a mental activity.

Sometimes when you have to make a decision there are several possibilities. You study them all, in the time allowed, and pick what seems to you to be the very best, based on all of the factors you are aware of at that moment. That is the possibility which you pick. Sometime later you suddenly label your decision or action a "mistake." How could that be when your decision was the "best" one at the time you made it?

* * * * *

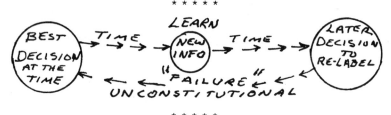

* * * * *

Something happened in the time between when you made your decision and the time you re-labeled it from "best" to "mistake." Well, you may have thought of something, remembered something, been told something, or observed the effect of your action. In any event, you acquired more information. That's called **learning**. So label it learning--and feel real good about it. Tell people about it so you'll remember it. If the act was OK when you did it, it's unconstitutional to make it wrong later. That's *ex post facto* labeling! Just like with the law, if it wasn't wrong when I did it, I'm not guilty.

On Guilt

I'm not a fan of guilt. It doesn't show me much. It can be used by you to control and manipulate me. Or I can use it to manipulate you. It isn't very enjoyable. You can use it on yourself to control your own behavior. You can warn yourself with self-talk such as, "If I did that I would feel so guilty I couldn't stand it." To me it's an obvious threat used to control the behavior of yourself or another person through the fear of feeling the pain and discomfort of guilt.

"You're being selfish" is probably the most common use of guilt. If I'm using that phrase on you, I want you to be so uncomfortable that you'll stop doing your thing and do what I want you to do. Of course you resent that. All those bad vibes add negativity to the environment. If you don't like being manipulated that way, just say, "Knock it off, you're not putting me on a guilt trip!"

I dislike guilt because it doesn't feel good, it's counter-productive and wastes energy. I much prefer a love-type emotion to a fear-based one. I also like freedom and choice as opposed to control and manipulation. I believe that one thing which makes us human is our ability to choose. If you take away my choices, you are de-humanizing me. But that's not all.

I think that guilt is unjustified and ineffective in improving human behavior. It's just a bummer! I don't remember any occasion when guilt improved anyone's behavior. Awareness of the consequences does a much better job of encouraging people to make right decisions.

Guilt is unjustified because everyone behaves in a way which seems correct, justified, fair, and sensible--based on all of their knowledge, assumptions, beliefs and expectations at the moment the decision was made. They may know a second after the action that it wasn't right, but at the moment of deciding it was their best choice based on the factors involved which they were aware of. So they did their best. They are not "bad," they are lacking in awareness.

Guilt really erodes the self esteem which is so essential to happiness and effectiveness. L. S. Barksdale, mechanical engineer, has been studying self esteem for 38 years. He's 78 now. At 40 when life is supposed to begin he was a millionaire but in extreme psychological pain. He turned his analytical mind onto the problem and has been working on it full time since. His conclusions are psychologically sound and practical. He established the Barksdale Foundation which publishes many excellent materials that can help a person improve his/her self esteem and get to feeling good about him/herself. (Barksdale Foundation, P. O. Box 187, Idyllwild, CA 92349).

The remorse of guilt often comes from not doing a "should" or doing a "shouldn't." Shoulds and shouldn'ts have a very subtle "you're not OK" message imbedded in them. Those messages are especially harmful to the self esteem. The shoulds are not an internal urging, they are external. They are the ideas of another person or organization being inflicted on one from the outside.

Rev. Henry Rucker of Chicago suggests an exercise which I think is helpful. Place a mirror somewhere in your home where you will pass it often. When going one way look at your reflection in the mirror and loudly say "**NOT GUILTY!**" When passing the other direction, look into your eyes and say "**I LOVE YOU, BABY!**"

On Giving and Receiving

I put these together because its difficult to give without someone receiving. We are a society that has the habit of thinking in opposites. Good/bad, right/wrong, true/false, black/white, conservative/liberal, capitalism/communism, rich/poor, giving/receiving. We tend to attach "good" or "evil" impressions to these opposites. What we like we call "good," what we don't like we call "bad."

We are also very competitive. Winning is good, losing is bad. Winning is being the "best," and that leaves losing to be the "worst." I think that the win/lose, good/bad dimension has crept into giving and receiving. Giving is greater so receiving has to be "lesser."

There is a rumor going around that, "It is more blessed to give than to receive." This idea triggers our competitive desire to be top-dog, to be the giver, the good guy, the winner, the strong one, not the weak one.

* * * * *

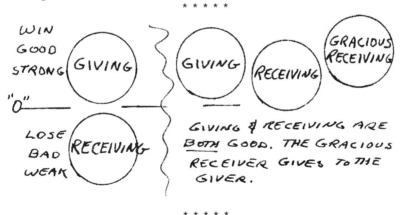

WIN
GOOD
STRONG   GIVING

"0"

LOSE
BAD   RECEIVING
WEAK

GIVING   RECEIVING   GRACIOUS RECEIVING

GIVING & RECEIVING ARE BOTH GOOD. THE GRACIOUS RECEIVER GIVES TO THE GIVER.

* * * * *

Some receivers really feel this "inferior" aspect of the receiving. They don't like receiving. "Oh, you shouldn't have!" (You're

101

darn right I shouldn't have--and next time I won't!) They act a bit insulted, as if you had called them "weak." Or you sense an immediate weight of obligation on their shoulders, the need to reciprocate, to "get even." Sometimes they may act embarrassed as if they did not deserve to be treated with such kindness. Others are instantly suspicious that you are going to ask a favor of them or sell them insurance, Amway products, brushes, Avon or Tupperware.

Giving may be "more blessed," but it certainly can be frustrating at times. There are a lot of frustrated givers out there along with many uncomfortable receivers.

Those two problems could become one solution if we could all decide that receiving is a great activity. It doesn't diminish our worth, or make us a loser, or weak, or evil. We deserve to feel good. That's everyone's goal in life. Besides, when you can receive graciously and comfortably, you give pleasure to the giver. Then the receiver is also a giver and you can both feel good.

So why not be cooperative instead of so competitive? It may still be more blessed to give than to receive, but just barely.

Giving/receiving are not opposites. They are by their very nature inseparable. (If you desperately need a receiver, I can give you one, **me**! Then I'm the giver.) Giving and receiving are a joint project in which both parties can and should feel good.

On Worry

We humans are a creative bunch. It seems to be our nature. We pour mental energy into our creation by thinking about, talking about and visualizing that which we want to create. It could be a painting, a statue, a song, a flower arrangement, a new soup, a unique business arrangement, or new racing stripes on our hot-rod car. Pour enough mental energy into the project along with some physical effort and, presto, what was once imaginary becomes real. It exists. It has been created.

This summer in the southeast, people have been pouring mental energy into visualizing rain to overcome the terrible drought conditions there. They have been praying for rain. In both the creative process and the visualization used in prayer, the outcome is one which is wanted and **desired**. The mental process used in creativity and prayer are powerful forces. And, like most powerful forces, they can be used or misused.

An example of the misuse of the power of the creative process is **worry**. In worrying we are thinking about, talking about and visualizing that which is **feared**. We have inadvertently set the creative process in action, but have applied it to what we don't want.

Some people act as if worrying about something keeps it from happening. The opposite is more likely. The self-fulfilling prophecy and the placebo effect are evidence that what we expect, believe (faith?), and visualize tend to come true. The experts in tennis, golf, and the olympic athletes know all about visualization.

Sometimes we see worry as our civic duty or a parental responsibility. "Of course I worry about a nuclear holocaust, I'm a conscientious citizen." One mother told me, "Of course I worry about my daughter, I love her very much!" That seems to me like **fear** is masquerading as **caring** and **love**. It's better to visualize what you want and move toward it than to visualize what you fear and try to escape from it. Worrying is a powerful, self-defeating process. Besides, it doesn't feel good.

Just how powerful is the imagination? Look around you. How much do you see that once existed only in someone's mind? This book, the chair, your clothes, the building, its furnishings, your car, your watch, etc., etc. In one sense we are still using this power to create our universe and our environment--for better or for worse. If we start with desire, it's for better. If we start with fear, it's for worse.

You can choose between better or worse for your contribution. It's **your** mind. Work to control it. Take charge of it. Be aware. Imagine a tiny replica of yourself perched up there on your shoulder taking note of what goes on in your head and what comes out of your mouth. You'd be surprised! If what you hear is fear-based then "cancel-cancel" that bit of mental activity and substitute a desire-based activity. Replace the negative with a positive. Then pat yourself on the back for your good work. (See The Big Lie, Sec. II). You'll be glad you did. You'll have more energy, be healthier and live in a better environment.

Worry is a form of fear, and all forms of fear produce fatigue. A man who has learned not to feel fear will find the fatigue of daily life enormously diminished.

Bertrand Russell

Worry affects the circulation, the heart, the glands, the whole nervous system, and profoundly affects the health.

Charles Mayo, MD.

Fear is an acid which is pumped into one's atmosphere. It causes mental, moral and spiritual asphyxiation, and sometimes death; death to energy and growth.

Horace Fletcher

Worrying is a fear-filled creative process which includes thinking about, talking about and visualizing loss, defeat, failure, trauma and chaos. It is a dangerous activity because it sets up scripts, programs and expectations which may be the beginning of a self-fulfilling prophecy. A bummer.

Wally Johnston

On Praise

Praise and approval are often thought of as creating good feelings. Not true for everyone. I've read a couple of research reports which indicate that 65 to 66% of the people didn't like praise. In order to praise you, I would have to have evaluated and judged you. And if I can set myself up to judge your goodness and worth, I can give myself the power to judge your shortcomings. If you'll notice in any courtroom, the judge always sits higher than the judgee. The judgee is low man on the totem pole. Not a great feeling. For many people, to be evaluated is threatening. Many of the teachers in Texas felt threatened recently when they were required to take a test to evaluate their knowledge and skills.

Praise can be used to lay an obligation on you, which is likely to increase your stress level. Have you ever been praised thusly? "You always do such a good job. I know we can rely on you." (Can you feel yourself grinding your teeth?)

Praise isn't all negative, even with the threat of judgment and the obligation. The approval part **does** feel good. We all need approval or love in order to survive.

Teachers, especially, like to use praise to motivate students and make them feel good. Once addicted to that external approval, the students need it just like any other "fix." And they like to receive it. In fact, they may have to have it or they are unhappy. This addiction to external approval makes people dependent. Being dependent makes them vulnerable to the whims of others. Not a relaxing position to be in. (Many teachers are also addicted to praise and expect the principal to supply the "fix.")

Since a person needs a certain amount of love and approval, I recommend an increase in self-approval. An honest pat on the back can feel just as good coming from yourself. I have to tell you another story. Correction, I **want** to tell you a story.

I had been teaching Human Relations to a class of teachers. We had covered "praise" just the week before. One beautiful soul, a 4th grade teacher, told her story about self approval and its effect. She had just finished doing the bulletin board in her classroom. She stepped back, looked at it, patted herself on the back, and said out loud to nobody in particular, "I did a good job. I like that!" The kids noticed. They talked about it. That afternoon while doing his math, one boy stopped, laid his pencil down, patted himself on the back, smiled, grabbed his pencil again and went on to check the next problem. Self motivation. Felt good. Not vulnerable. So don't let the "conceit" label deter you from self approval.

* * * * *

THREAT LEVEL OF DIFFERENT TYPES OF PRAISE.
(MOST THREATENING)

PERSONAL WORTH → "YOU ARE A GOOD PERSON."

PERFORMANCE → "YOU DID A GREAT JOB."

APPEARANCE → "YOU LOOK NICE TODAY."

POSSESSIONS → "THAT'S A BEAUTIFUL CAR YOU HAVE."

SHARING MY FEELING/REACTION → "IT'S A JOY TO WATCH YOU."

RECOGNIZING AND ENCOURAGING SELF-APPROVAL. GIVING PERMISSION TO ENGAGE IN SELF-APPROVAL. → "I CAN SEE THAT YOU ARE PLEASED WITH YOURSELF." (LEAST)

* * * * *

I envision a sort of continuum or hierarchy of the threat which is involved in praise or approval. Self approval is the least threatening, while the approval or judging of the personal worth of the individual is the most threatening. Judging of performance, appearance, or possessions tends to decrease the threat in that order.

It is even less threatening to a person if you will share the feeling reaction which you experience. "I enjoy knowing you." "I'm happy to see the way you performed." "You are like a breath of fresh air to me." This type of sharing will tend to bring two people closer together than the praise which sets up a judge and a judgee. The threat is eliminated, sharing takes place and everyone feels better.

Love Is Limited?

It's quite painful to think that love is limited. If my brother gets a lot then there isn't enough left for me. The Smothers brothers acted as if their mother's love was limited and they were competing for what there was of it. "Mother always did love you more than me." This scarcity concept is baloney. Love isn't like gold or platinum. Love can be created in abundance. It's more like a muscle--the more you exercise it, the more there is.

Our next door neighbor in Lincoln had this concept. During WW II our nest emptied very rapidly. Five sons went into military service and two daughters married servicemen and left home. Just baby sister was left with Mom. Dad died in September of that same year, 1943.

The neighbor had the concept that love is limited so that the total love you have is distributed amongst those whom you love. My sister reported on the discussion. The neighbor lady had one son. She explained very carefully to Mom how lucky Mom was. If she, the neighbor lady, should lose her only son in the war it would be a very devastating experience. However, if Mom lost a son in the war it wouldn't hurt so much. Presumably, since Mom had six sons, it would only hurt 1/6th as much because her love was divided six ways. Mom didn't buy it. But as usual she was very patient and only said, "She means well."

As it turned out, all the sons and sons-in-law came back in one piece. And the neighbor's only son was turned down by the draft. Much ado about nothing--except that it makes me a good illustration 43 years later.

Love is limited? Baloney! It need not be rationed. And there's no need to worry if the one who loves you also cares about other people. So just relax and enjoy life.

Spit Out the Apple!

One morning recently I woke up with original sin on my mind. (I can hear some of you saying, "Just another dirty old man!") It didn't have anything to do with sex, directly. I was passing through that state called hypnogogic reverie or hypnopompic reverie. (I can't remember which one is going to sleep and which one is waking up.) Anyway, it's the state you are in when the brainwaves are about 8 hertz or cycles per second. That's the border between the alpha region and the theta brainwave region. It's a very creative state. Thomas Edison is reported to have taken about a dozen naps a day. He had a lot of trips through that state. No wonder he had about 12,000 patented inventions. It's too bad daydreaming got such a bad reputation. That cut off a lot of creativity. But, back to the story.

I reviewed what "sin" is. It has two meanings for me. The first meaning is separation. Separation between people. My picture is that we think we are all individual fingers and haven't discovered that we are all attached to the same hand. The other meaning for me is that sin is missing the mark, off target, derailed, off the track or off the beam. (Wrong behavior is due to a limited awareness.)

Then I remembered our compulsion to judge nearly everything. Good/evil, right/wrong, true/false, black/white, liberal/ conservative, etc., etc.

I'm not speaking here of evaluating or becoming aware of what exists. Awareness of reality is necessary in order to evaluate situations and make decisions and choices. But that is not rejection of others. It's my judging/rejecting which seems to separate us. I judge that you are evil, or at least not OK. Then I separate myself from you. I reject you on the basis of my judgment. I refuse to accept you. You don't come up to my high standards. Now I've judged, which is a "no-no." And I've also created a separation which is sin. I've really made a mess of things. It's no wonder that I got myself kicked out of paradise (Genesis 3). The consequences were automatic, considering my behavior.

Beneath all this mess I thought I saw the reason. I **really believe** that I have absolute knowledge of good and evil! Aha! If I hadn't eaten the apple, the forbidden fruit of the tree of knowledge of good and evil, then I wouldn't even **know** the difference between good and evil. **All** of God's world would still be paradise. I wouldn't have this compulsion to judge/reject and separate myself from my brothers and sisters.

Adam said that Eve talked him into it. Eve said the serpent was to blame. As you can see, the blame game goes back a long way.

Then I remembered that one man's meat is another man's poison, and that one man's sin is another man's learning experience. Who am I to judge? Can I give up my knowledge of good and evil? Maybe it isn't too late to **spit out the apple!**

An Acorn or a Chevrolet?

Many of the discussions that I have observed and engaged in revolve around an assumption about the nature of people and learning. Some believe that people are molded and formed from the outside, as a Chevrolet, while others believe that people, like acorns, have inside them all of the ingredients with which to become an oak tree. The Chevrolet group agrees with John Locke who saw little people as a tabula rasa, an erased tablet, or a blank slate. The job of parents, schools or the church is to write on the slate or tablet what ought to be written there to make an educated, decent human being. The expert who has all of the knowledge stands and faces the blank slates (or empty heads) who sit in straight rows and are made to pay attention so that their heads can be filled with the right stuff, as determined by the experts. I wonder if the experts were born with blank slates, and if so, who wrote on their blank slates. And the blank slate before that, and on and on.

Sometimes those little empty heads aren't so empty. They ask questions such as Why? Where did I come from? What keeps my body warm? Where will I go when I die? What is the difference between good and evil? Just what is life? What is learning? Who am I? Out of the mouths of babes often flows wisdom--much more wisdom than can be found on a blank slate.

As you have probably sensed, I'm not a Locke man or a Chevrolet type. I know that a lot of technical information can be transmitted from the front of a room to a class in a very efficient manner. I'm also sure that what is taught isn't always the same thing as what is learned. I remember the story of the cornflakes.

A young adolescent boy had reached the bravado stage. One morning at the breakfast table he impatiently yelled, "Pass the damn cornflakes!" Wanting to teach the boy not to swear at the table, the father stood up, reached across the table and gave his son the back of his hand. After breakfast, the father, being a good educator, asked the boy what he had learned. The boy responded, "I'm sure as hell not going to eat any more cornflakes!" The father hit the boy physically, but he missed the mark educationally.

Myself, I'm an acorn person. The acorn needs the right climate and environment. Then with very little guidance it knows how to become its own oak tree. To make an oak tree you don't start with raw materials and smelt, mold, hammer, grind and paint it into a specific model. The blueprint is on the **inside** of a living being, the **outside** of the non-living object. The job of education includes facilitating that growth from the inside out as well as from the outside in. I like what Kahlil Gibran says about the teacher in THE PROPHET:

> *No man can reveal to you aught but that which already lies half asleep in the dawning of your knowledge.. . . .*
> *If he is indeed wise he does not bid you enter the house of his wisdom, but rather leads you to the threshold of your own mind.*

I believe that one way to "lead you to the threshold of your own mind" is to share my experiences and feelings, then you listen for the resonance, the "click," that tells you if it is true for you. Explore your own inner blueprint. If you think outer space is interesting, you may find that inner space is even more exciting!

It Can't Be:
The Self-defeating Quirk of the Human Race

My mother-in-law admitted recently that she thought I was crazy back in the 1940's when I would talk about people going to the moon. Then we went to the moon, so I wasn't crazy. Now I talk about other things and she must think I'm crazy again.

"It can't be" has to do with our belief/disbelief system. A man in Los Angeles, Bill Jenkins, has a radio show on KABC. He calls his show the "Open Mind." He speaks of our "reality box" in describing the belief/disbelief system. If the idea fits inside the reality box, then "it can be." If it lies outside the reality box, then "it can't be." Inside is a belief, outside is the disbelief.

In doing workshops I sometimes spoke on human potential and the amazing things which human beings are reported to have done. As I get more and more "far out" someone will giggle. Then I know that I've passed their "giggle point." Going to the moon was beyond my mother-in-law's giggle point in 1945.

The gullible one, who believes everything is true, gets caught up in fads, or even cults. That's a waste of time and leads to lots of disappointments, which don't feel good. At the other extreme, the closed mind has committed a form of intellectual suicide, misses a lot of exciting developments, never learns as much as he/she might, and thus gets cheated out of some good feelings that seem to be inherent in the learning process. I think we need a box entitled "it might be."

The "it can't be" people have slowed our progress from time to time. Copernicus was not well received when he suggested that the earth was **not** the center of the universe. His ideas did not set well with the religious authorities of his day. Galileo didn't do so well either. Jesus promoted the idea that love can work and he was nailed to a tree.

Robert Goddard was a "lunatic" out in the fields shooting rockets into the air back in the 1920's. "It couldn't be. You can't escape from the earth; you can't go to the moon." In WW II the Germans were using Goddard's formulas to send V-2 rockets to London. We had to get Von Braun, the German scientist, to bring Goddard's technical knowledge back to this country. Goddard's widow got 2 or 3 million dollars in patent rights a few years ago. Then we named the space center after Goddard. Sometimes we're so damn smart that we act stupidly. We could have lost that war. Our "It can't be" attitude toward Goddard's work nearly did us in.

Beliefs die hard. When the TV pictures were sent back from our early space explorations, "The Earth Is Flat Society" was actively claiming that the pictures were a communist plot!

I can remember being in the 8th grade. The teacher had been to a conference and heard about some French psychologist who claimed that people would be helped by saying to themselves, "Every day in every way I'm getting better and better." We laughed. (I wonder why I remember that incident.)

Now sales managers, medical doctors, psychologists and especially sports psychologists are using verbal affirmations and visualizations. It might be to enhance sales, or healing, or the performance of pro athletes and olympic gold medalists. We lost more than 50 years by being so smart.

In the 1950's Wilhelm Reich was working with what he called Orgone energy. He was declared a fraud, equipment destroyed, books burned. We were "protected" by an agency of the government. I think that Reich may very well be our next Goddard. The idea of a mysterious energy has been with us for 5,000 years and probably won't go away. John White wrote an article for Psychic magazine which was published in the January/February, 1976 issue. The article was entitled "X Energy & Consciousness." It listed ancient sources such as the Chinese Chi, Japanese Ki, the prana of the yogis, and mana from Hawaii. Some energies were identified by Indian tribes, Eskimos, Pygmies, Aborigines, etc. As modern sources, Paracelsus, Mesmer, Blavatsky, Steiner, McDougall, Bergson,

Jung, Reich, and Freud all made their contributions. There were more than 45 energies listed in the article. The first century Christians called it "Holy Spirit." Sounds a bit like "love," doesn't it? That idea won't die. Maybe we should take an "it might be" attitude toward it and investigate it scientifically.

However some "scientists" have a very small reality box. They look at some reported phenomenon and state authoritatively that "It can't be." No experiments, no observations, just the conclusion. That isn't science. That's dogma, which is an opinion held as absolute truth by a religious sect. That kind of a "scientist" isn't looking for truth, he's already found it. Yes, Virginia, you can belong to a religious sect and call it "science."

As for me, the only way that I can be certain that "It can't be," is for me to **know** everything in the universe and **know** that there is nothing more. I may be arrogant, but I'm not **that** arrogant!

Beliefs and Their Incredible Power

While walking through the stacks of the library at Winona State University one day, I caught sight of a book. The title just "jumped" out at me. I wasn't looking for anything related to physiology. It was a report of the Third Annual Symposium of the Kaiser Foundation Hospitals in Northern California held in San Francisco. It was entitled THE PHYSIOLOGY OF EMOTIONS, edited by Simon and others. I checked it out.

I was already aware of the fact that what you believe about yourself has a strong influence on your behavior or performance. If you believe you're a winner, you probably are. If you believe you're a loser, it is even more probable that you are. If you see yourself as a $50,000 a year salesperson you are likely to reach that total, if it is at all possible to do in your territory. If you have a $100,000 territory, you're still likely to reach only $50,000, because that's what you believe you are, a $50,000 salesperson. If you think you are a poor speller, you will misspell about the same number of words per page. We seem to have a need to be consistent with our beliefs.

For years we all **knew** that a human being could not possibly run a mile in less than four minutes. Roger Bannister destroyed that belief. In the year following his breaking of the 4-minute barrier dozens of runners also broke that barrier. So, I already knew that beliefs were powerful, but this book added a new dimension to my awareness.

The section presented by Charles C. Herbert, MD, was the one which caught my attention. He quotes reports from a wide variety of sources: medical, psychiatric, psychosomatic, pathological, and cultural.

The first report concerned an experiment on a criminal who had been condemned to death by public hanging. A famous physician was allowed to perform an experiment in the prison. The criminal had consented to be bled to death prior to the date of his hanging. He was blindfolded, strapped to a table in spread-eagle fashion. A vessel of water had been hidden under each corner of the table. Four pans were placed, one at each corner to catch the "blood." The wrists and ankles were scratched, but not deeply enough to draw blood. However, as each scratch was made, the valve on the vessel of water at that corner was opened enough to drip, drip into the pan. The criminal, who could hear the dripping, "believed that his blood was escaping." He died without the loss of one drop of blood.

In 1943 in London 600 people were crowded into a bomb shelter. A bomb exploded nearby. The lights went out. Somebody stumbled noisily on the stairs. Pitch dark. No yelling or crying, just fear. When the lights came on 200 were dead. "Post mortems revealed no significant anatomical changes in the victims." The **belief** that they would die killed one-third of the group.

Another report was about an assistant who was hated by the students at college. They had some sort of kangaroo court and condemned him. He was held with his head on a chopping block, eyes blindfolded. One student "made the noise of a swinging axe, another dropped a warm, wet cloth on his neck. The assistant died instantly."

I listened to a report by a visiting medical doctor at Mayo Clinic. He told about a dermatology experiment in Japan. Thirteen subjects were told that a branch of fresh leaves was poison ivy. It wasn't, but eleven got a rash. In the next experiment the subjects were exposed to a branch of leaves which was presented as harmless. It was really poison ivy, but only two broke out in a rash.

The placebo effect is more evidence of the power of beliefs. Some 30-40% of people who take a placebo, such as distilled water or a sugar pill, believing that it is a medicine which will help, are actually helped.

And if you believe that you are unable to do something, you are probably right. In fact, you probably won't even try.

Yes, beliefs can make you well, make you ill, slow you down or even kill you. So, if you believe that life is a gift to enjoy, go ahead and feel good! Take charge!

On Pessimism and Optimism

The optimist, forever looking on the bright side said, "I believe that this is the best of all worlds." The pessimist, forever focusing on the darker side responded, "I'm afraid you're right."

We see and experience what we are tuned to and what we expect. A pessimist and an optimist could walk across the same pasture. One would enjoy the fresh air, birds, flowers, breeze and blue sky. The other would be afraid of the "cow pies" and would be looking out for them. The pessimist would probably spot patches of bare ground in the distance, thus seeing more CS (that's similar to BS) than was actually there.

The optimist, acting on his/her **desire** to enjoy the world and the time, would do just that, and enjoy it. The pessimist, having some **fear** of stepping in the CS, would tread carefully avoiding the hazards and arrive on the other side relieved. But the pessimist would have missed a nice experience and a bit of joy. If the optimist stepped in a "pie" the pessimist could get some joy out of saying, "I told you so!" To the optimist it's not catastrophic, just an inconvenience.

The pessimist will usually notice the bad news, the juiciest scandals, the most corrupt acts and the worst crimes. That's the kind of world the pessimist inhabits. But there must be a good feeling involved in seemingly proving oneself to be right about the world being an awful place.

On Religion

When it comes to taking charge of one's feelings, the area of religion is a mixed bag. We all have an assortment of powerful emotional memories from major events and early events in our lives. Many of those memories include religious overtones. For some, religion means a source of love and comfort, a guide to living well. For others religion is a source of guilt, an unlimited supply of "shoulds," or a tool of control through rules backed up by an immense amount of fear and worry should the rules be violated.

I had the thought once that if so much fear had been imbedded in me that I absolutely could not "sin" for fear of my own pain of guilt, then I'd have no choice but avoid all of the temptations of life. But if I had no choice, then I was like an animal, and I would be without morality. The paradox is that the organization which was trying to make me moral would destroy my morality. My ability to enjoy the gift of life would be diminished. And I'd be full of fear instead of love. In my book, God is love, not fear.

Religion is another inside/outside possibility. If God and His/Her Word are outside, someone needs to put it inside those of us who don't yet have it there. There are a lot of volunteers to do just that. Two volunteers visited us once. They had my wife backed into a corner of the kitchen when I got home for lunch. They told me that if I prayed, they **knew** what God would answer. They had a direct connection, a WATS line to God, so to speak. I thought if that was possible for them it was also possible for me. (I don't know what they'd do to God if He/She didn't come through as they said.)

The Book, the Bible, can be a great resource or a big "club" with which to threaten people. (One of the most interesting parts is how much God improved between the Old Testament and the New. He/She may still be improving.) If one believes that

God is everywhere that includes the insides of each of us. We can each have a spirit and be "inspired." So when I'm asked if I believe that the Bible is the word of God, I usually answer, "Probably, but not any more than the READER'S DIGEST." When I don't agree that they have the infallible truth in their left hand, the discussion usually ends.

I have never figured out why, if the Book was such a good idea, Jesus didn't write it himself, or at least dictate it. It is my fantasy that in his time Jesus insisted that His teachings **not** be written down, that He was talking about **love** and **spirit**, immaterial things. Recording the teachings would make them **material objects**. (I think that the teachings were not written down for 20, 40 or even 100 years. If Jesus **did** instruct his followers not to write down his teachings, 20 years seems like a reasonable time in which to forget **that** teaching.) Now there are so many material objects surrounding religion such as buildings, committees, budgets, doctrine, robes, etc., that the purpose of promoting love can be lost. After a grueling five hour committee meeting, it's difficult to remember that "God is love."

Religion is a "loaded" subject. The feeling/memories surrounding our experiences with religion and churches can make us very upset. If you take charge of your life and are brave enough to look at your experiences relating to religion, you might ask yourself these questions: Is this organization based on fear or love? Is the object to control me or set me free to grow? Do I feel like a "child of God" or as low as a worm? Which choice do I want to make?

It takes faith to question your faith. If your beliefs won't withstand questioning, they are questionable. If they stand up, you are on solid ground, and the feeling associated with your religion will be positive.

On Abortion

When I was young, abortion was an illegal solution, mostly for the unmarried girls who had "sinned" by engaging in pre-marital sex and getting pregnant. There were people around who would perform abortions. Even though it was illegal, it was often preferred to the lifelong condemnation by society. I guess you could say that on the good/evil scale they were about equal.

How things have changed through the years. Sex and having babies outside of marriage is accepted much more. Abortion is now legal, but to part of society, what is legal is the "sin." One segment of society is condemning another segment and calling them murderers and harassing them for doing what is legal. Sometimes it is even the "God is love" group and the "judge not" group that is judging and harassing. It's interesting, to say the least. I'm not at all sure what is right on this topic, but I promised to share, so I will.

I can remember thinking that abortion was "awful." Then I learned about how babies seem to die when they experience an environment with little or no loving and touching. Nothing physically wrong, they just died. My interpretation of that phenomenon was that Mother Nature, in her wisdom, placed a higher value on a loving environment than on life itself. It was as if it was better to abort the body or vehicle of the spirit than to force the spirit to continue in an unloving environment. I thought a lot about that one.

Then I read Raymond Moody's LIFE AFTER LIFE and got acquainted with Elisabeth Kubler-Ross and her research, and then read ten books on OOBE, the Out of Body Experience. Next came reports on "remote viewing" experiments. That's a lot of new stuff to synthesize.

One of my students, while relaxing using biofeedback, found his consciousness up in the corner of the room looking down on his body. Then my wife remembered when she was three years old and broke her arm. She still has a very clear picture in her mind. She can see her little body across the room standing by the kitchen table, biting on the corner. But she had not realized that she was out of her body. Her consciousness had to be across the room for her to see her body from that angle. If she had been in her body, behind her eyeballs, she would have seen the table top, not herself. Then came Bob Monroe's JOURNEYS OUT OF THE BODY in which he reported on his first 568 trips! It seemed like time to enlarge the reality box. There was too much to deny and too much to fit into the old box.

If pain, a near death experience, drugs and deep relaxation can place the consciousness outside the vehicle, then why can't the consciousness survive after the body deteriorates, or exist before the body forms? (You can probably substitute spirit, self, or soul for consciousness, depending on your belief system.)

About that time I read a book written by Ostrander and Schroeder entitled, PSYCHIC DISCOVERIES BEHIND THE IRON CURTAIN. It was full of things that wouldn't fit into the average reality box.

I remember the experiment which the Russians did with the mother rabbit and her babies. The mother was all wired up in the laboratory. The babies were taken out to sea in a submarine. The submarine submerged to a depth which was beyond radio contact. The babies were killed one at a time, the time being carefully recorded. On returning to the laboratory, it was found that the mother had experienced a violent physical reaction at the instant when each of her babies was killed. There was "communication" of some sort going on, and it seems to have been without the benefit of any "material" substance. Was it telepathic, spiritual, or transmission of thought (if rabbits can think)? Some form of exchange had taken place between mother rabbit and her babies. Maybe all mothers and babies can communicate on some level.

If the consciousness can exist inside the body, outside the body, and while the body is clinically dead, why can't the same consciousness exist before the body is formed, or while it is being formed? Maybe it is possible for a mother to have a type of communication with her unborn child.

If pre-birth communication of some sort is possible, why not try to use it? (Please don't say, "It can't be," unless you know all about the universe!) If it seems impossible to provide a loving environment for the baby, why not send that message to the consciousness of the unborn? Relax, meditate and send the message. Then wait for an impression. Maybe suggest a post-ponement of the birth.

Since having these ideas, I have worked with two pregnant women for whom motherhood at that time would have been devastating. I shared the idea with each of them. It made sense to both of them. They both had miscarriages. A sample of two doesn't prove a thing. But both women took charge of the situation, lovingly "conferred" with the other "party" involved, and arrived at a guilt-free solution without an abortion. It may have been a coincidence or a case of successful communication and feeling management.

On Suicide

I think it was Woody Allen who hit the nail on the head when he said that he had considered suicide, but he was afraid that it was only a temporary solution. I agree. It doesn't stop the psychological pain, it doesn't kill the consciousness, it only punishes and terminates the body. And the aftermath of pain and guilt in the survivors can be enormous.

I'm not talking about people who feel that their time has come and they prefer to take charge and decide on a dignified method before their energy and finances are drained through the tubes and wires of heroic measures which do more to prolong the suffering than to enhance the living. (I read a statistic the other day which said that 80% of our lifetime medical expenses occur in the last year. But how do you know which year is the last?) These people are not emotionally disturbed or in a lot of psychological pain. They are problem-solving and planning for an event which they are certain will occur, and probably soon.

It is the emotionally disturbed, those in severe mental anguish, those who are trying to end the pain through killing the body that I'm talking about. They can not think clearly, if at all. They are trying to get rid of a problem, and at that time see death as the only solution. They need to talk about the pain, the fear, the humiliation, the discouragement, or whatever brought on the attempt at suicide. They may not know how to talk about their feelings. They may not even have the vocabulary for it. They may believe that nobody cares enough to listen or try to understand. If you can be calm and full of compassion, you might say, "It **really hurts**. It's frightening to hurt so much-- and to be so alone." If you can put into words what they are feeling at that time, they will begin to feel understood. They will begin to feel less frightened and alone. Your calmness can be contagious, can engulf them. You might even imagine that bubble of light surrounding them. I remember listening to a counseling tape by Dr. Carl Rogers. For two hours and 20 minutes he attempted to put into words what his client was feeling. The client remained silent. Finally the dam broke and the man, a patient in a mental hospital, decided that Carl did care and could be trusted. Then he spoke for the **first time** in more than **16 years**.

I know you are not Carl Rogers, and neither am I, but you don't have to have a doctor's degree to care about a human being. Some people would say to "show that you care." I say just care, and it **will** show. But not all suicide threats can be treated with loving understanding.

Some threats are outright attempts at manipulation. "Love me and do what I say, or I'll kill myself." Other attempts are an effort to send a message. One lady had tried three times to kill herself when she came to me. It finally came out that all she was trying to communicate was that she wanted her parents to love her. My instant response was, "My God, lady, you can talk plainer than that! Ask them to love you." Her parents were so tense that they didn't know whether to visit her or stay away. If they visited, they didn't know whether to talk or be silent. If they talked they didn't know what to talk about. They didn't know if they should be solemn or happy. They didn't know what might trigger attempt number four. I think the lady is still alive and I hope that her communication with her parents has improved.

A friend of mine told me about his attempt at suicide when he was about 27 years old. He was married, had a family, a job which was going nowhere with a company that was on the skids, working with people whom he saw as "losers." He was quite overwhelmed. He more or less absent-mindedly took his .22 rifle with him as he walked into the woods. These were the same woods where he had so much enjoyed squirrel hunting as a young boy. It was autumn and the leaves were beginning to turn color. He said he "came to" with the rifle placed at his temple and his thumb on the trigger. Then he noticed the trees and the beauty. And then the memories of his boyhood flooded his mind. Something clicked. "I can be that happy again." He put the gun down, full of determination to get help. He told me he would have walked the 50 miles to the next town through sh-- up to his chin just to see a psychiatrist. Today he is happier than ever. Income is in six figures. He still has the rifle. And he remembers well the day something clicked and he chose life.

If you feel suicidal, check out that negative self-talk. Take charge and change "I can't stand it" to "Hmm, this is interesting. I wonder what I'm to learn from this experience." (If that doesn't work, put on your Nikes and try to walk yourself to death.) If nobody loves you, ask someone to care about you, no matter how awful you may seem to be. There are people out there in the world who are ready to care, and with no strings attached. Look for them. You could be surprised. There are also people out there who will be willing to take advantage of you so don't be surprised by them either.

On Unexplained Suicides

Sometimes there is a suicide for which absolutely no reason can be found. That's when I suspect the "invisibles."

One of the problems with death is that to the dead it seems so much like living that they are not aware that they no longer have their own bodies. Franklin Loehr's book, DIARY AFTER DEATH, gives such an example. Henry was walking back to his office after lunch when he noticed that the people he was meeting on the sidewalk seemed to be startled by what they saw behind him. He was in front of the Field Building on LaSalle Street in Chicago, about 50 feet from the entrance to his office. Being curious, he turned around and saw that a man was lying there. He walked back and saw that the man was about his size, had a hat like his and even a briefcase just like his. He watched as his body was carried to an ambulance. Then he proceeded to his office, but nobody paid any attention to him. Death may not be the same for everyone but this is how Henry Clements reported his death through psychic channeling to Rev. Loehr who is a medium. But then if 100 of us went to Philadelphia and wrote back about it, those letters would all be different, wouldn't they? I've read dozens of accounts in which the dead do not realize they are dead.

It is my hunch that some of those unexplained suicides for which absolutely no reason can be imagined are, in fact, another attempt at suicide by an invisible who successfully killed him/herself in a previous suicide attempt, but doesn't realize it. By being caught up in the body and energy system of a living person, the invisible, earth-bound spirit mistakenly believes he/she is alive and wanting to die. If the invisible can gain control of the body, he/she might make another suicide attempt. That this is possible is documented in Wickland's THIRTY YEARS AMONG THE DEAD.

Dr. Wickland's case happened November 15, 1906 in

Chicago. (We seem to be having a run on Chicago!) Mrs. Wickland, while in trance fell to the floor and remained comatose for some time. When the spirit entity finally spoke through the voice of Mrs. Wickland (a medium) she acted as though in great pain, repeatedly saying, "Why didn't I take more carbolic acid? I wanted to die; I'm so tired of living."

They learned that the spirit entity was (or had been) Mary Rose of 202 South Green Street and had one son. She could not remember what day it was (the 15th) but when asked if it was Nov. 15th, she said, "No, that is next week." After explaining to the former Mrs. Rose that she had succeeded in her attempt and was on the other side, "her spiritual sight opened slightly and she saw dimly the spirit figure of her grandmother, who had come to take her to the spirit world."

When they checked out the address, they found that Mrs. Rose had lived there, and the son still lived there. They were told that she had been taken to the Cook County Hospital the previous week and had died there. A check at the hospital showed that she had been admitted Nov. 7 and had died on Nov. 8 of carbolic acid poisoning. (Case No. 341106)

Woody Allen, I think you were right. Suicide is only a temporary solution. If you enrolled in this "school of life" to learn a particular lesson, it would be best to hang in there (bad choice of words for an essay on suicide!) until you learn it or you may be held-over to repeat the grade.

The Inner Guidance System

I've talked a lot about not letting others control you or manipulate you. So just where do you get your direction, your guidance? In recent years there has been exciting evidence that we do have definite resources within ourselves to keep each one of us on his/her unique track. If we each march to a different drummer, we need to know how to listen to that beat.

Many years ago I read a book by a Dr. Smiley Blanton entitled LOVE OR PERISH. Just the title was enough to get my attention. It registered with me. Dr. Blanton headed a center for religion and psychiatry in New York City. He said that "The kingdom of God is within you." In a way that made sense. If God is everywhere, then He/She must be in me. Otherwise God is everywhere **except** in me and there is a "me-shaped" hole in the universe. The former made more sense than the latter. Then Blanton finished his statement. He added, "It's your unconscious." This was refreshing news to me since Freud had given the unconscious mind (UCS) such a bad name--full of sex and selfishness. It clicked. I wanted to believe it and it felt good.

Then along came Eugene T. Gendlin, PhD, and his book called FOCUSING. He describes a process that sounds like your conscious mind is listening to your UCS mind. When something is "eating on you," deep in the gut, it won't let go until your conscious mind gets the message. Then there is a "felt shift" as something releases and lets go.

Have you ever left the house with the slight tugging or nagging feeling in the gut that you have forgotten something? Purse, billfold, keys, lock the front door, close the garage, turn off the oven? If you find the item, or your companion confirms that you did take care of it, then the tugging lets go. Sometimes you just have to go back to be sure before the feeling will leave.

In therapy Gendlin found that there is no real growth unless you get a "felt shift" and the gut releases the tension. An article in the Brain/Mind Bulletin suggests that there is a shift in the brainwave pattern at the time of the release. I speculate that, if the most accurate model of the brain is the hologram, then the felt shift in the gut, and the shift in brainwaves will be accompanied by a change in the holographic picture of the world in your head and the world will never look exactly the same again. The holographic brain model reminds me of some research reported by Joseph Chilton Pearce in THE MAGICAL CHILD. Pearce reports that cats raised from birth in an environment containing only vertical lines, when placed in a normal environment would run into the horizontal rungs of the chairs, just as if they had nothing horizontal in their holographic model of the world and so couldn't see the rungs. I guess to the cats, horizontals "just can't be." They are not in the cats' belief systems. Horizontal lines and objects lie outside the cats' reality boxes and beyond their giggle points.

Just a few years ago I read about Dr. Ernest Hilgard, the man from Stanford who wrote an introductory psychology textbook which had about 30 revisions. After Hilgard retired he studied hypnosis. He identified a part of the mind with which he could communicate while the conscious mind was asleep. He called it the "hidden observer." As nearly as I can recall, this hidden observer is in charge of the "back burner." When you put things on the back burner and let them simmer, you can get some answers or insights later that have been "cooked up" while your conscious mind was doing other things. It is probably that part which takes over after you visualize a perfect performance and guides you through it while the conscious mind just stays out of the way. This hidden observer reminded me of a story I had heard about Robert Louis Stevenson. It was reported that he talked to the "Brownies in his head," asking them to awaken him the next morning with a story on his mind for him to write out.

The hidden observer doesn't use judgment. It's more like a computer, "garbage in, garbage out." I think it must be the part that stays awake all night while your conscious mind sleeps and awakens you at the time you want. (Maybe you can't do that but I'll bet you have a grandparent who can.)

This year I read about the most exciting piece of the puzzle. A lot of material on multiple personalities seemed to be popping up in front of me in articles, newsletters and books. One of the books, MINDS IN MANY PIECES, is by Ralph B. Allison, MD, a psychiatrist from Morro Bay, California. He has had many patients with multiple personalities. This is quite rare. Usually about one or two to a career is all that can be expected. With a larger group he could begin to draw some generalizations. Using hypnosis he found what he called the "Inner Self Helper." Rather than an alter personality he calls it an "entity." These entities regard themselves as spiritual agents or guides. They attempt to guide the person toward sound mental health. They can report all of the experiences of all the personalities and even make helpful suggestions to the psychiatrist. It sounds a little bit like the "still small voice," or the guardian angel, or "be still and know that I am God," or "the kingdom of God is within you."

Some of those words are really loaded. Undoubtedly Dr. Allison's findings will lie outside the "reality box" of many of his colleagues. (The Aug. 18, 1986 issue of the BRAIN/MIND BULLETIN reports that while 95% of the Americans polled believe in God, only 43% of the American Psychiatric Association and just 5% of the American Psychological Association believe in God.)

However, no matter how many people disbelieve the possibility, that in itself doesn't make Dr. Allison's findings untrue. I hope that his research won't be treated in the same way as Robert Goddard's rocketry research. (See "It Can't Be," this section). We tend to give our best leaders a very hard time before we make them heroes.

In any event, I am encouraged that there is the possibility that we just might decide to explore the "Inner Guidance System" and find better ways to live with each other, ourselves and the world. It could lead us to more joy and less pain.

Section IV
A Philosophy of Life

A philosophy of life is made up of many different elements. The mottos, quotes, learnings, religious teachings, belief/disbelief system, and assumptions which are made about people and the world all go into it.

All of this material serves as a foundation from which we operate as we live our lives consciously, or more often, unconsciously. Taking charge of one's life definitely includes taking a look at this basic but often overlooked foundation.

On Having A Philosophy of Life

Everyone has one, a philosophy of life, a guide by which to live and make decisions, or to justify the decisions already made. It is a set of assumptions and rules. It is unique to each person. It comes from various experiences and the conclusions, if any, which follow the experience. The philosophy of life and the belief system are closely related. Bits and pieces come from quotations, famous sayings, TV commercials, folk lore, and Bible verses. We are not always aware of these bits and pieces. I will include my collection of quotations, many of which may sound familiar to you. There may even be some which you use to guide your life. These bits and pieces of "wisdom" can have a large effect on the quality of your life. Two relevant bits are "Know thyself" and "The unexamined life isn't worth living." Also, "The unlived life isn't worth examining!"

Some of our early conclusions are not conducive to happiness. Some are very self-defeating. Most go back to the early years or to times of great emotional upset when the mind could not think clearly. Now, with a calm, mature mind you can re-think those conclusions and arrive at a second opinion which can add to the quality of life.

When I was a management psychologist in St. Louis, I interviewed over 100 executives. A part of the interview asked about the earliest memories of these men. (That's correct, they were all men. Sorry about that.) I was amazed that the themes of the early experiences of these men were still evident in their adult lives.

If the early memories included death, violence, and accidents, they were very likely to view the world as a dangerous place. The expectations of danger tended to be fulfilled in the later experiences of that individual. My favorite was a man whose earliest memory was one of achievement. At about age three he climbed to the very top of the windmill. It was a very exhilarating memory for him. (Fortunately, nobody screamed and planted a fear of heights in him! There must have been a very nervous parent or two for a while.) This man was a real achiever.

My most unfavorite executive was a man who kept a file of all the hurts, insults and put-downs that had happened to him. He had been carrying in his billfold for 12 years a memo which he had interpreted in a hurtful way. A large part of one file drawer was full of such letters and memos. He knew that the world was a lousy place and that he would always be a victim. And he was right, of course. But he was unhappy. He needed to do some reexamination of his philosophy.

I reexamined some of my philosophy. I was indoctrinated with a "work ethic" in my early years. Pop used to say, "Wallace, it's all right to wear out the knees of your overalls, but you'd better not wear out the seat." To loaf was sinful. (The devil finds work for idle hands, you know.) I remember thinking that if I worked like a horse and produced like a machine, then I deserved the dignity and respect of a human. Then I had a chance to go to heaven. Somehow that didn't make sense to me. I decided that if heaven was for horses I could live without it.

My father's approach to life seemed to be to suffer now, play later. You'll get your reward in the sweet by-and-by. The other choice was to play now and suffer later. (That wasn't much of a choice either. If you decided to play now you couldn't enjoy it much knowing that you would have to suffer later.) This was not an unusual philosophy. Only occasionally could you find a person who believed in enjoying the gift of life. And they were looked down upon, as if to find joy, one somehow had to be "sinning."

The philosophy of life is a sort of undergirding, a foundation, like the foundation of your house. (How often do you inspect that?) I picture the foundation as being made of stones, some large, some small, some even gravel-size. The big stones are questions such as:

Who am I?
What is the purpose of life?
What is the nature of man: good, evil, both, or neutral?

136

Is there a God or higher power?
Are we accidental or God's creation?
What happens at death?
What is eternal life?
Is it going on now?
What about reincarnation?
If there is a God, is He/She inside of me or external?
Was I consciouness first, and then became flesh, or was I flesh first and then consciousness entered my body?
To what, if anything should I dedicate my life?

Some of the smaller stones as I see the foundation would include such concepts as learning, growth, behavior, human relationships, thinking and believing. These stones get mixed with the gravel and bits and pieces which make up the mortar for the foundation on which we base our lives.

I think your life can have more meaning and satisfaction if you take time to identify your foundation. Inspect each stone, then accept it, reject it, replace it, or modify it to suit your current beliefs. I will share with you what I wrote in 1972, 1976 and 1986. I trust that you won't adopt **my** philosophy. If any of it "clicks" it was already **yours**.

* * * * *

I BELIEVE: October 3, 1972

That what a person BELIEVES and FEELS about himself affects what he sees and how he feels about the people around him.

That people BEHAVE in a way which seems JUSTIFIED to them in light of what they see, believe, feel, assume or are aware.

That one of the most severe LIMITATIONS of many people is what they believe they CANNOT do--and by "not doing" they prove themselves correct, live down to their PREJUDICE and fulfill their own prophecies.

That ways of interacting are developed to meet certain needs, but these behavior patterns become habits and may remain long after that need disappears.

That people can and usually will change in the proper climate.

That change involves the EXCITEMENT of the new as well as a FEAR of the unknown.

That changing, learning and growing are LIFELONG

activities and the best defense against boredom.

That learning and growing, becoming more adequate, becoming more effective and realizing one's potential are rewarding experiences--they feel good and add meaning to one's life.

That a person will get more satisfaction from accomplishing the objective which HE/SHE helps select than from striving to achieve someone else's purpose.

That self-knowledge allows a person to make more realistic and more effective choices; that self-knowledge is the best basis for self-direction.

That MAKING CHOICES is a human function, and that to unnecessarily deny choices is to dehumanize the person.

That self-disclosure, self-exploration and self-examination lead to self-understanding; which leads to self-acceptance; which leads to acceptance of others; which leads to improved interpersonal relations; which leads to effective communication; which leads to a responsive organization; which can benefit society.

* * * * *

I BELIEVE   March 5, 1976

That I have a choice. I can choose not to choose.

That the past, or the **effects** of the past, can be changed by choosing to reinterpret the event or by choosing an alternate way of perceiving the event.

That most psychological pain is self-inflicted.

That psychological pain can be reduced or eliminated--if I know how, want to, and choose to change it.

That an excess of feeling hinders the functioning of the cognitive processes.

That my thoughts affect my feelings and my feelings affect my behavior.

That my thoughts (tapes, scripts, internal dialog, etc.) are habits which have been learned, and can be unlearned.

That my thought habits can affect the functioning of my body, my posture, my energy level and my physical health.

That my mind can communicate with and influence nearly every cell in my body.

That my subconscious mind takes literal directives from my

verbalizations and my visualizations even when I really do not desire it to do so. I can, through being unaware, program myself for pain, disappointment, illness, failure, self-defeat, accidents or death.

That touch transmits an energy as yet unexplained.

That negative thoughts and visualizations create a measurable deficiency in energy which retards growth.

That there is only one fear: Un-cope-ability.

That satisfaction makes life a joy and satisfaction comes from the assumption of responsibility for self.

That the purpose of this existence and of future existences is to grow toward maturity, toward acceptance of and respect for all forms of life, toward compassion and love.

* * * * *

As I reviewed those items I found nothing with which I would argue today. As I went through each item, I enjoyed recalling again the research reports which I had read that led to those beliefs. (Sometimes I'm amazed at the "stuff" I have stumbled into through the years!) Now for a look at the present.

* * * * *

I BELIEVE   September 12, 1986

That life is what we make it.

That we can focus on the "good" or the "bad" parts of the world and that is the world we will experience.

That what we believe to be true about the world really is true for us.

That what we project into the world with our attitudes, assumptions, beliefs and expectations are reflected back to us by all living beings.

That this reflection is an inevitable consequence, similar to the reflection of a mirror.

That the Creative Intelligence of the universe will allow us to create more and more destructive weapons as we project more and more fear into the world and attempt to find safety by manufacturing destruction in order to produce more fear.

That the world can work, but the mirror is inevitable. Fear begets fear and love begets love.

That humans are energy systems which serve as centers of

conscious awareness.

That energy can not be destroyed, so human personality is an energy system forever.

That human consciousness is capable of creating a difference in the universe.

That there are other realms in the universe in addition to this reality.

That things not yet understood, the "occult," are the **most** important subjects for scientific investigation.

That if both science and religion honestly seek the truth, they will arrive at very similar conclusions.

That truth will not remain static since creation continues through the mental energy of consciousness.

That if either religion or science believes that it has found the TRUTH, it will become rigid and stagnant and defend old " truths," sometimes visciously.

That the human body and mind are both created to be self-healing, and what we call symptoms are often evidence of the efforts of the mind or body to heal itself.

That the energy system and center of conscious awareness which is the human also contains a source of knowledge, wisdom and spiritual guidance.

That an energy field, a life-field or L-Field surrounds the human and is related to the mystery of life.

That the L-Field, when detected by instrumentation or Kirlian photography will predict physical changes in the body prior to their appearance.

That thoughts and/or emotions are also energy and constitute a thought field or T-Field.

That the thoughts and emotions, the T-Field, can affect the L-Field which seems to be the electrical/magnetic blueprint of the physical body.

That these relationships are a logical system for studying the healing effects of positive thought as well as the illness-producing effects of negative thought related to illness.

That love is an energy which heals and enhances growth and can be directed by human consciousness.

That this love energy has been discovered more than 40

times in the past 5,000 years.

That this idea will not go away (even if ignored) whether it is called love, or Holy Spirit, or God, or prana, or orgone, or ki, or whatever.

That love will work better in human relationships than fear, threat and manipulation.

That somehow a form of "tough love" is worth a try in national relationships.

* * * * *

To all of that I'd like to add that, if I find that I'm wrong, it would be very approriate for me to rejoice because of the learning rather than to be ashamed or embarrassed because of the "mistake."

(If the L-Field idea intrigues you, look up Harold Saxton Burr from Yale about 50 years ago, or Sir Jagadis Bose of India. Currently, Valerie Hunt has a book coming out on the measurement of the energy system surrounding people.)

We have been dealing with some pretty heavy stones in the foundation. Now it is time for some of the lighter pebbles that go into the mortar and fit between the biggies. I'll bet you recognize a lot of these. Examine the list to determine if any are influencing your current philosophy. Some are contradictory. Some will be true for you, some will be false.

QUOTATIONS

A bird in the hand is worth two in the bush.
A fool and his money are soon parted.
A house is made of brick and stone but a home is made of love alone.
A leopard doesn't change his spots.
A penny saved is a penny earned.
A quitter never wins and a winner never quits.
A rolling stone gathers no moss.
A sinner can reform but stupid is forever.
A stitch in time saves nine.
A woman's place is in the home.
A woman's place is in the House or the Senate.
Absence makes the heart grow fonder.
All generalizations are false, including this one.
All is fair in love and war.
All that glitters is not gold.
All that is required for evil to succeed is that good men do nothing.

Always remember that you are unique, just like everyone else.
An eye for an eye and a tooth for a tooth.
An idle mind is the devil's workshop.
Anything worth doing is worth doing well.
As the twig is bent, so is the tree inclined.
As you sow, so shall you reap.
Ask not what your country can do for you, but what you can do for your country.
Be ye therefore perfect as your father in heaven is perfect.
Beauty is in the eye of the beholder.
Beauty is only skin deep.
Better safe than sorry.
Boys will be boys.
Children should be seen and not heard.
Cleanliness is next to godliness.
Cold hands, warm heart.
Diamonds are a girl's best friend.
Disappointments are caused by expectations.
Don't burn your bridges behind you.
Don't cast your pearls before swine.
Don't count your chickens before they're hatched.
Don't cross the bridge till you come to it.
Don't cry over spilled milk.
Don't get mad, get even.
Don't push the river.
Don't put all your eggs in one basket.
Don't sweat the small stuff.
Don't start vast projects with half vast ideas.
Don't throw out the baby with the bath.
Early to bed, early to rise makes a man healthy, wealthy and wise.
Eat it up, wear it out, make it do, or do without.
Experience is what you get when you don't get what you want.
Finders keepers, losers weepers.
Give them an inch and they'll take a mile.
Go with the flow.
Good fences make good neighbors.
Happiness is an inside job.
Haste makes waste.
He who hesitates is lost.
He who laughs last laughs best.
Hell hath no fury like a woman scorned.
Honesty is the best policy.
Honor thy father and mother.
Housework is like stringing beads with no knot at the end of the thread.
If at first you don't succeed, try, try again.
If everything is coming your way, you are probably in the wrong lane.
If it ain't broke, don't fix it.
If the shoe fits, wear it.
If you're not for me, you are against me.
It is more blessed to give than to receive.

It matters not if you win or lose, but how you played the game.
It takes a heap of living to make a house a home.
It takes one to know one.
It takes money to make money.
Jesus said to be kind. He didn't say be stupid.
Judge not that ye be not judged.
Know thyself.
Let sleeping dogs lie.
Let the buyer beware.
Living well is the best revenge.
Loneliness is one thing you can't walk away from.
Look before you leap.
Love conquers all.
Love is blind.
Love is never having to say "I'm sorry."
Love it or leave it.
Love thy neighbor as thy self.
Make hay while the sun shines.
Make your mother proud.
Man does not live by bread alone.
Man works from sun to sun, but woman's work is never done.
Moderation in all things.
Money is the root of all evil.
Nary a slip between the cup and the lip.
Necessity is the mother of invention.
Never leave till tomorrow what you can do today.
No guts, no glory.
No man is an island.
No one can make you feel inferior without your permission.
No pain, no gain.
Nothing is certain but death and taxes.
Nothing succeeds like success.
Nothing ventured, nothing gained.
Only a mediocre person is always at his best.
Once burned, shame on you. Twice burned, shame on me.
One man's meat is another man's poison.
One man's trash is another man's treasure.
One person's floor is another person's ceiling.
One swallow doesn't make a summer.
Out of sight, out of mind.
Pain is inevitable, but suffering is optional.
Paralysis through analysis.
Power corrupts. Absolute power corrupts absolutely.
Pride goeth before a fall.
Progress is our most important product.
Put up or shut up.
Put your money where your mouth is.
Robbing Peter to pay Paul.
Someone ought to write a book: "When to oversee and when to overlook."
Sometimes it is better to ask for forgiveness than to ask for permission.

Spare the rod and spoil the child.
Stay alive as long as you live.
Sticks and stones will break my bones but words will never harm me.
Still water runs deep.
Strike while the iron is hot.
Suicide is the severest form of self criticism.
Sugar and spice and everything nice, that's what little girls are made of.
Sugar will catch more flies than vinegar.
Talk is cheap.
That is like the pot calling the kettle black.
The bigger they come the harder they fall.
The devil finds work for idle hands.
The early bird gets the worm.
The hurryer I go, the behinder I get.
The Lord helps those who help themselves.
The Lord loves a cheerful giver.
The sooner you fall behind, the more time you have to catch up.
The squeaky wheel gets the grease.
The unexamined life is not worth living.
The unlived life is not worth examining.
The watched tea kettle never boils.
There's more than one way to skin a cat.
There is nothing more frightening than ignorance in action.
There is nothing to fear but fear itself.
Time is money.
Time is nature's way of keeping everything from happening at once.
Time heals all wounds.
Time wounds all heels.
To err is human, to forgive divine.
To the victor go the spoils.
To thine own self be true.
Too many cooks spoil the broth.
Variety is the spice of life.
Waste not, want not.
We get too soon old and too late smart.
What goes around comes around.
What you resist will persist.
What you see is what you get.
When my ship comes in I'll probably be at the airport.
When the cat's away, the mice will play.
When the going gets tough, the tough get going.
Where there's smoke, there's fire.
Wisdom is knowing the difference between pulling your weight and throwing it around.
Yard by yard life is hard. Inch by inch life's a cinch.
You can lead a horse to water but you can't make him drink.
You can't get blood out of a turnip.
You can't have your cake and eat it too.
You can't judge a book by its cover.
You can't make a silk purse out of a sow's ear.

You can't teach an old dog new tricks.
You get what you pay for.
You never can tell the depth of the well by the length of the handle on the pump.
You shouldn't feel that way.
You are never too old to learn.
You only go around once in life so you gotta grab all the gusto you can get.

I hope you have enjoyed looking over my shoulder as I have examined some of my own foundation and attempted to state what I believe. More than that, I hope that you have been encouraged to take charge of your philosophy of life and put into words those things which **you** believe. Doing a thorough examination of your philosophical foundation will be enjoyable. You may find some places which need attention.

Section V Quick Fixes

Here I've listed some of the quick fixes for the minor snags that trip up a lot of us in our day-to-day living. The observations, suggestions and ideas are short enough to recall (hopefully), yet long enough to be adequately descriptive.

You may find yourself recalling the suggestion a day later, an hour later, or a minute later. As the time shortens, that's progress. Eventually, if you keep practicing, you will remember the "fix" at the time you need it. That will feel good!

Quick Fixes for Minor Snags

Watch how you talk to yourself or you may be "hung by the tongue."

For "you make me angry" substitute "I'm upsetting myself."

"Have to" makes me feel coerced. "Choose to" reminds me of my power.

"Can't" disables me. "Won't" keeps me in control of my life. I'm not "unemployed," I'm "available."

It's not a catastrophe, it's only an inconvenience. (Dr. Albert Ellis)

Please don't blame me for not knowing what you refuse to tell me.

When there is a problem, ask, "Who is upset?" Whoever is upset owns the problem. The solution lies within the one with the problem. The upset **is** the problem. (Dr. Tom Gordon, PARENT EFFECTIVENESS TRAINING.)

For "Ain't it awful?" try, "Isn't this interesting!"

For "I can't stand it!" try, "Wonder what I'll learn from this."

It's not a failure until I say it's a failure!

I'll be responsible for my intentions, but I will not be responsible for the way in which you misinterpret my intentions.

Just because I'm asked a question, doesn't mean that I'm compelled to produce an answer.

Just because I can see an answer, that doesn't make it my problem.

Good/bad, right/wrong, true/false? I don't know. I'm free. I don't have to have an opinion.

Are you "shoulding" on yourself? You really shouldn't!

Disappointments can only come from expectations. Who is in charge of yours?

Insecurity is caused by trying to find security, which doesn't exist. Frustrating, isn't it? Try substituting flexibility for security.

Rule 1: Survive. Rule 2: Follow Rule 1.

11th Commandment: Do the best you can with what you know and the materials you have to work with within the time allowed.

Fear of making a "mistake" leads to "paralysis through analysis" and leaves you stuck. You have to act to get experience, and experience is the stuff from which you learn.

Boredom is an uncomfortable feeling created by your inner wisdom to get you off your duff so you can start learning something, doing something or helping others.

Be glad when you're told, "It's all in your head," because that's where the solution is also.

When asked a personal question which you'd rather not answer, you can say, "I hope you'll forgive me for not answering your question. I've already forgiven you for asking it."

When asked to serve on a committee, don't assume that you must serve unless you can come up with a good excuse. Just say, "Give me some time to try and find a reason to say yes." If they keep pushing, say, "I know it's **your** goal to have me on the committee, but unless I can find a reason to make it **my** goal I'm sure I would resent it. And we wouldn't want that between us, would we?"

Formula for good therapy: Find someone you care about and who cares for you. Then get the following:

4 hugs to survive

8 hugs to function

12 hugs to grow.

Mixing those energy fields will be good for both of you. (And remember, you can't hug with nuclear arms.)

Know that, short of being physically attacked, you cause your own upsets. To find out how you are doing it ask yourself these questions:

1. What am I upset about?

2. Why does that upset me?

3. Why do I believe my answer to #2?

4. What could I believe that would be just as true and wouldn't upset me?

5. What is keeping me from believing my answer to #4?

There are no mistakes, there are only learning experiences.

I am not what I do. I am the doer.

If I'm right, I don't have to yell. If I'm wrong, it won't help.

The universe is my classroom. It is trying to teach me something which I need to know. It is not picking on me. The universe wants me to enjoy myself so that I'll fill it with good vibes.

What difference will it make 100 years from now?

Do you know why angels fly? They take themselves so lightly! Taking yourself too seriously makes you a drag. Then you can't get off the ground.

Section VI
Affirmations

An affirmation is a statement about yourself which either is true, or you want to become true. A famous quotation says that as a man thinketh, so is he. So just expand on that a bit and make it read, "as I think and say and see, so I become." You'll think up the best affirmations for yourself. I suggest these only as a place to start.

When you make out your list, remember to use the positive form. For example, say, "I walk gracefully," rather than, "I won't stumble." Also, affirm only that which is in your control. (Don't use, "My mother-in-law loves me.") You may want to stick your list on your refrigerator door. You may decide to get some relaxing background music and read your list onto a cassette tape to which you can listen morning and evening. The tape can be 15 or 20 minutes long. You should listen to it twice a day for three weeks before you expect the affirmations to start becoming a part of you. After that, listen each week, or as needed.

To listen to your tape, find a quiet place and get comfortable. You'll need something to focus your mind on, such as your breathing, or the fireplace. Just say "I am" as you inhale slowly and say "reeelaxxxed" as you exhale. It will help if you breathe with your abdomen. That will increase the oxygen supply and help your body keep itself healthy. The more deeply you can relax and the more clearly you can see yourself enjoying your affirmation, the more effective it will become. **Know** that relaxation is possible for you.

If you'd like a ready-made tape, send to Bob Griswold at Effective Learning Systems, Inc., 5221 Edina Ind. Blvd., Edina, MN 55435. His catalog lists more than 30 tapes on a wide variety of subjects such as worry, health, sobriety, pain relief, blood pressure, weight loss, smoking control, deep relaxation, PMS, how to be happy, and even on taking charge of your life. There are many sources, but I've used these. They are good.

AFFIRMATIONS FOR TAKING CHARGE OF MY LIFE

I do my own thinking.
I make my own decisions.
I accept a task when I see a good reason to do so.
I say NO without feeling guilty.
I say YES only if I find a good reason.
Each decision I make is my best one at that time. When I know more, I'll make better choices.
A mistake is a sign I've just learned something.
I do things which are worth doing.
Anything worth doing is worth doing imperfectly the first time.
A failure is just an unmet expectation.
The world responds to my needs.
The world is just as it should be.
My world is my classroom. I learn.
I am in charge of my life.
I am at peace.

AFFIRMATIONS FOR MANAGING MY FEELINGS

I am free to describe my feelings.
I enjoy expressing what I feel.
I am free to laugh and show joy.
I am glad that I can describe my anger, and know that it hurts no one.
I enjoy showing my love.
I am free to cry and be sad.
By crying, I release my pain and hurt.
I am in charge of my feelings.
I decide what events will mean to me.
I change my past by allowing myself a second opinion, a second interpretation.
I release my regrets from the past.
I release all fears of the future.
This instant, now, I am calm and at peace with myself and the world.

AFFIRMATIONS FOR PROMOTING PHYSICAL HEALTH

I feel calm and quiet.
My arms and hands are heavy and warm.
My feet and legs are heavy and warm.
My shoulders are relaxed.
My face and neck are relaxed.
I breathe deeply and slowly.
My heart beats strong and rhythmically.
My digestive system works smoothly.
My eyes focus correctly, my vision is clear.
My hearing is clear and accurate.
My joints and vertabrae are strong and flexible.
My muscles are strong. I enjoy using them.
My period is regular and comfortable.
My skin is clear and smooth.
My body is at (or approaching) its normal, healthy weight.
My sex organs function well and give me pleasure.
I appreciate the way my body works and the way it heals itself.
I care for my body with proper food, rest and exercise.
I love and appreciate my body.

AFFIRMATIONS FOR IDENTITY AND SELF-ESTEEM

I belong, I am a part of the universe.
I am unique, precious, one of a kind.
I can cope. I am adequate.
I approve of myself.
I do the things which will help me like myself.
The people who know me best like me very much.
I have made the decision to care for myself.
I choose to love myself.

RESOURCES

Ralph B. Allison, MD. MINDS IN MANY PIECES
Barksdale Foundation (Self Esteem), PO Box 187, Idyllwild, CA 92349
Smiley Blanton, MD. LOVE OR PERISH
Harold Bloomfield, MD. MAKING PEACE WITH YOUR PARENTS
H. Boswell. MASTER GUIDE TO PSYCHISM
John Diamond, MD. YOUR BODY DOESN'T LIE
John Diamond, MD. LIFE FORCE
Albert Ellis. (Many books on Rational Emotive Therapy)
Marilyn Ferguson, Ed. BRAIN/MIND BULLETIN, PO Box 70457,
    Pasadena, CA 91107
Eugene T. Gendlin. FOCUSING
Kahlil Gibran. THE PROPHET
Gerald Jampolsky, MD. LOVE IS LETTING GO OF FEAR
Bill Jenkins. KABC Radio (LA) "OPEN MIND"
Daniel Keyes. THE MINDS OF BILLY MILLIGAN
Jess Lair. SEX: IF I DIDN'T LAUGH I'D CRY
Lawrence LeShan. YOU CAN FIGHT FOR YOUR LIFE
Franklin Loehr. DIARY AFTER DEATH
Robert Monroe. JOURNEYS OUT OF THE BODY
Ostrander & Schroeder. PSYCHIC DISCOVERIES BEHIND THE
    IRON CURTAIN
John N. Ott. HEALTH AND LIGHT
Joseph Chilton Pearce. THE MAGICAL CHILD
Flora Rheta Schreiber. SYBIL
David Sheinkin, MD, et al. FOOD, MIND & MOOD
A. Simon, MD. THE PHYSIOLOGY OF EMOTIONS
Pitirim Sorokin. THE WAYS AND POWER OF LOVE
Fred Soyka. THE ION EFFECT
Thigpen & Cleckley. THREE FACES OF EVE
John White. "X-Energy & Consciousness," in PSYCHIC, Janu-
    ary/February, 1976
Carl A. Wickland, MD. THIRTY YEARS AMONG THE DEAD

ABOUT THE AUTHOR

Wally Johnston brings to this book the synthesis of a wide range of preparation and experience. Born on a Nebraska farm, the sixth child in a sibship of ten, Wally was educated in the Lincoln schools. He served as editor of the Jackson High School newspaper, president of student council, and earned two letters in football before graduating in 1939.

Following a year at Agriculture College, University of Nebraska, and three semesters at Nebraska Wesleyan, he served as a weather observer in Sheridan, WY.

His military career began with ten months in the Navy V-5 pilot training program after which he received flight training in the Army Air Corps. He completed pilot training and was commissioned a Second Lieutenant in 1944. Wally served as a B-25 instructor pilot and was trained in B-24's, and Navy PBY's. He was deputy A-2 (Intelligence) for a fighter wing in Okinawa for 10 months before returning to civilian life in 1947 to continue his education at Nebraska Wesleyan.

Wally completed the BA at Wesleyan in 1948, with a major in physics, a minor in math, and certification as a secondary school science teacher. He was a teacher/principal at Stromsburg, Nebraska, 1948-51 while earning credits toward a masters degree in school administration at U. of Nebraska and flying C-46's on weekends at Offutt AFB. The degree was not completed as Wally was recalled to active duty as an Air Force reservist for the Korean conflict.

The Air Force tour included training in survival and nuclear weapons; aeronautical ratings of navigator, bombardier, radar observer, senior pilot and command pilot; duty in Guam, Alaska, Japan, England, Germany and Africa; and assignment as instructor pilot in B-29's and B-47's with the Strategic Air Command (SAC).

Wally left the Air Force in 1959 with his B-47 Observer after organizing a corporation and raising funds to test the feasibility of a new method of drying lumber. A test plant was built in Bend, Oregon. The method proved to be not feasible. However, the co-managers developed and patented a novel method of drying wood *veneer. The corporation went broke before the veneer drying method could be marketed and Wally returned to the education field in 1962 at nearby Sisters, Oregon, as Superintendent of Schools. He served there for two years before receiving a National Defense Education Act (NDEA) fellowship to the University of South Dakota, Vermillion.*

At Vermillion ('64 to '67), Wally completed the MA and EdD in Educational Psychology before moving to Winona State in Minnesota. After one year in Winona, he spent a year as a management psychologist in St. Louis, MO, before returning to Winona State. At WSU Wally had a joint appointment as counselor and counselor educator, serving as assistant, associate and full professor before retiring in 1980 as professor emeritus.

While still at WSU Wally went into private practice as a Licensed Consulting Psychologist in Rochester, MN, where he continued until 1984 when he retired. While in Rochester he designed and built an innovative energy efficient home.

Post doctoral training in biofeedback at Menninger Foundation, PARENT EF-FECTIVENESS TRAINING with Tom Gordon, workshops on death and dying with Elisabeth Kubler-Ross, MD, and workshops on psychic phenomena broadened Wally's experiences. A faculty improvement grant in 1975 permitted him to attend a conference on consciousness and suggestology which opened more new vistas and led to a sabbatical leave in 1977. While on sabbatical, he and his wife and daughter traveled 13,000 miles in 33 states and Canada visiting 60 places where interesting new developments were taking place, all in the pursuit of his favorite game, the cosmic jig-saw puzzle.

Wally's wife, Ardis, accompanied him not only on the sabbatical, but through the other 42 years and more than 30 homes. They have four sons, two daughters and six grandchildren.

The metaphors utilized in his writing reflect the diversity of background and experience as he shares with us the fruits of his 65 years as innovator, scholar, therapist and teacher with the universe as his classroom.

*Although I have no **personal** knowledge of how he spent his first 6 years, I can vouch for much of the rest of it!*

RUTH L. JOHNSTON, PhD, RN